C000234382

THE NEW
OLD HOUSE

historic & modern
architecture
combined

MARC KRISTAL

foreword by GIL SCHAFER III

abrams, new york

FOREWORD
gil schafer III

SOME OF THE MOST INTERESTING CONVERSATIONS occur when there are opposing points of view—as long as they are undertaken with intelligence and civility. So it is with buildings, too, and that "conversation" is at the heart of what intrigues Marc Kristal in this book. Roaming both sides of the Atlantic, he has sought out—and now shares with us—a delightfully diverse collection of examples of the intriguing dialogue that can happen between history and modernity, when the two are brought together in a skillful architectural intervention.

It shouldn't surprise you that a writer would be interested in stories, and Marc is no exception. As I learned when we worked together on my own book, Marc has a particular gift for "reading" buildings and uncovering what it is they are trying to say. As well, he knows how to articulate beautifully the stories one can find within a structure: to put you in the place where it is, and to help you understand the forces that shaped it. Such stories are the cornerstone of his strategy in selecting the eighteen uniquely compelling houses for this book. In each, the architect and the client (sometimes one and the same) made powerful connections to the original character of a house, which they retained and celebrated while bringing the structure into the present. And the variety of geographical locations, historical contexts, and architectural solutions makes for a wonderful read.

As an architect working within a historical design context for nearly thirty years, I am always intrigued by the possibilities an old building offers for contemporary life—and have remained enthusiastic about architectural interventions rendered in a modern mode, when they're executed inventively *and* elegantly and when they demonstrate a clear understanding of the essence of the historic original. Marc's fascination with a house's narrative is well matched to my own, and we share a belief that residences in particular are part of a continuum and have the opportunity to be reinvented with each new inhabitant. The extension of that continuum that a new resident brings to a piece of historic architecture is all the more revitalizing if it is the result of weaving together both old and new. The acid test is, of course, whether or not the outcome is more livable, and beautiful, than what existed before. I think you will find that to be the case with each of the houses that follow—and I heartily encourage you to join me in the journey of discovery that this book offers.

And besides, who doesn't love a story about second chances?

OPPOSITE: Longbranch, Key Peninsula, Washington, designed by Jim Olson.

INTRODUCTION

ON MY DESK, AS I WRITE, ARE THE TOOLS OF MY TRADE — elements belonging to the here and now — and reminders of the past. Some, for example the figure carved from a block of redwood by my father, speak to sentiment. Others — the commemorative champagne glass I received at the 1979 dedication of the JFK presidential library (filled with push pins), or the clay pot that once held dried laurel (and now paper clips) purchased at a shop on the Île Saint-Louis — combine memory and function, and flatter my self-image (that of a well-traveled man of parts). The cork covering the desktop was cut from a bulletin board in a long-ago studio and so blends history and utility with a third component, design. And there is more: objects, images, furnishings, all coalescing into a place to work, a selective self-portrait, a record of a life. Like a home, my workroom is a mix of things bought, collected, and inherited, expressions of my present-day tastes and an appendix of the history from which those tastes emerged. And like many of us, my everyday narrative includes the simultaneity of the present and past — the moment, and everything that stands behind it — a story told by the details, individually and collectively, that comprise the environment I recognize as mine.

Which brings us to the idea of combining historic and contemporary architecture — of giving old buildings new life. There are sound, explicable reasons to do so. With a flexible approach to preservation, many aesthetically valuable, still-useful places can play a part in the modern world while sustaining the pleasures of the past. As reusing an existing structure is one of the "greenest" of building practices, finding effective strategies for so doing contributes to the global drive for sustainability. The preservation of buildings for their larger historic (as opposed to strictly aesthetic) value also means that locations — indeed, entire city- and landscapes — that are rich in meaning can

retain their influence (even if they're not so nice, like the so-called dictatorship urbanism found in parts of the former Soviet Bloc).

At the institutional scale, a well-conceived addition to a historic structure can amplify, extend, contradict, or comment upon the narrative begun by the original. A vivid instance is C. F. Møller Architects's twenty-first-century Darwin Centre, a colossal, cocoon-like object appended to the 1881 Natural History Museum in London; though it could not be more different in style from its predecessor, the structure, which was built to hold the museum's collection of specimens (seventeen million insects, three million plants), as well as offices and exhibition spaces, suggests the vastness of the enterprise and uses a form from the natural world to express the idea of protection and transformation. And while buildings that can only be fixed via new construction are ubiquitous, they often occasion the most imaginative solutions. Norman Foster's faceted 2006 Hearst Tower exemplifies this: His forty-six-floor "green" high-rise, the first in New York City, juts from Joseph Urban's cast-stone 1928 Art Deco base; the original design called for a skyscraper, which was scotched by the onset of the Great Depression, and Foster effectively completed the building, transforming Urban's six-story structure into an atrium-like podium, and sustainably answering the Hearst Corporation's need for space.

As Foster's design suggests, complicated problems can be the best generators of design solutions, whether aesthetic, programmatic, performance-driven, or all three. This points to a truism I've heard from many practitioners: The best way to get good work from an architect is to provide not a blank canvas but something requiring a response. In this vein, the creative polymath Mattia Bonetti told me some years ago that the French tradition of state patronage made artists "sleepy" because they knew they'd be supported no matter what,

a sentiment amplified by Erwan Bouroullec, who admitted that he and his brother Ronan—two of France's most prolific product designers—worked better yoked to a client's demands than with complete creative freedom. If nothing else, the givens of an old building will set an architect's mind in motion.

And perhaps ironically, but above all: Protecting history is a quintessentially modern act. Observing that some of the first architectural preservation laws in France were introduced immediately following the revolution, the architect Rem Koolhaas noted that "preservation is part of the repertoire of modernity."

Yet reinventing an old house engages a somewhat different muscle; often, it goes beyond what is sensible and can be explained into the aforementioned realm of narrative, the moment-by-moment influence of history on the present. You can, of course, choose a residence for practical reasons—X number of kids require X number of bedrooms, the size of the garage derives from the amount of cars. Or you can renovate, altering the program while maintaining the optics. Many people appreciate the character and details of a Colonial farmstead or Greek Revival townhouse, to cite two examples, yet most such buildings lack up-to-date kitchens, adjoining breakfast spaces, and family rooms—the holy trinity of contemporary living—and so are entirely unsuited to the requirements of today; to compensate, there are practices that specialize in delivering the architectural equivalent of a jailhouse beating, breaking and rearranging the bones of charming but outmoded houses while leaving no stylistic welts.

But few things are more personal, and emotional, than the idea of home, and an old house can also speak to us on what the novelist Ralph Ellison called "the lower frequencies"—those aspects of our nature, often as not unconscious, that are attracted to certain engagements because of the possibilities they present. It is, in fact, like choosing a mate. You can pick a person because he/she, as the saying goes, looks good on paper. Or you can be drawn to something inchoate, a pheromone that suggests that interleaving oneself with a particular other will be at once individually strengthening and mutually enriching—a better me, a better you, and, not least, an entirely new, exceptional *us*.

ABOVE LEFT: C. F. Møller Architects' contemporary Darwin Centre, appended to the 1881 landmark Waterhouse building, at London's Natural History Museum.
ABOVE RIGHT: Norman Foster's Hearst Tower in Manhattan rises from an Art Deco podium by Joseph Urban.

9

So it can be with a house. Just as the braiding of the practical and personal in my workroom produced a condition in which my imagination is encouraged by layers of experience, so too can a historic dwelling inspire you to respond to its promise with a new design that builds on an existing narrative—to create an architectural marriage that supports, sustains, and brings out the best. The landscape architect Laurie Olin has described cities as "accumulations of partialities": layers of urbanistic endeavor, compiled over decades or centuries, collectively comprising a single, multivarious experience. Hybrid homes, it might be said, are urban conditions in miniature—accumulations of partialities that, if brought into balance, produce a journey through a simultaneous past and present, wherein history informs modernity, combines its story with ours, and which we daily, warmly enrich with the ongoing tale of our own inhabitation.

My interest in architectural narrative—in the stories buildings tell, and how one learns to decipher them—grew out of a lifelong attraction to the movies. As a child, I was a great consumer of Hollywood classics, which were not at all difficult to follow and offered straightforward messages of the love-conquers-all, crime-doesn't-pay variety. As I got older, however, and began to sample the foreign food of European cinema, I ran into trouble. The narratives of many of the films that were presented to me as masterpieces were often entirely confusing or obscure. *Breathless, The Seventh Seal, The Discreet Charm of the Bourgeoisie, Last Year at Marienbad . . .* Certainly they *seemed* great, and I was fascinated. But what, exactly, were these movies about? What, to paraphrase Samuel Beckett, were they *meant to mean?*

When one is in a country and doesn't know the language, one pays extra-close attention in the hope of picking up clues. That was my approach with foreign films, and gradually I came to understand that in the best of these pictures, I was experiencing something timeless that was being related in a way that was individual. My breakthrough moment came as I watched the end of Federico Fellini's autobiographical *I Vitelloni,* in which the protagonist, leaving his hometown forever, suddenly imagines his train passing through the bedrooms of his sleeping parents and friends. Witnessing this exquisitely poignant scene, I realized that, though Fellini's magical-realist method of conveying his character's feelings was personal ("Fellini-esque"), his message was universal—and that the maestro's unique artistic language was precisely what elevated the moment.

Decades later, after working as a screenwriter, I switched to architecture and design journalism, and found myself struggling with a new version of that language problem. I interviewed dozens of practitioners who patiently explained their approach to this or that

project. Yet while I liked much of what I saw, and developed an understanding of how buildings were made, I wasn't getting inside these creations in the way I could get inside a movie. The reason, I felt, was ignorance—I had insufficient knowledge of the language to understand what these structures had to tell.

The fog began to lift when I became familiar with the Venice-born architect Carlo Scarpa, who did much of his work in Italy's Veneto region. Scarpa wore many hats—he was a design consultant to the Venini glassworks in the thirties and forties—but it is his museum renovations, notably the Gallerie dell'Accademia in Venice, Galleria Regionale della Sicilia in Palermo, and most famously the Museo di Castelvecchio in Verona, for which he is best known. In each case, Scarpa was engaged to create new exhibition spaces within historic buildings, and each provoked, as one writer put it, "profound reflections on the relationship between ancient and modern and their coexistence."

Many of Scarpa's ideas would be familiar to anyone who has visited a well-done adaptive reuse project, among them clearly drawn distinctions between old and new; the repurposing of historical artifacts; the insertion of new rooms within old ones; the exposure of a structure's layers to give clues to its history; and the introduction of elegantly designed and crafted architectural objects to invest spaces with detail and the presence, within history, of modernity. (The 2007 book *Carlo Scarpa: Architecture and Design* offers an excellent introduction to his oeuvre.) Yet for all their refined elegance—their exceptional richness and beauty—it was an additional component in Scarpa's museum projects that commanded my attention: his ability to embed enigmatic yet palpable narratives in the buildings, stories that even those with a limited understanding of architecture could recognize and appreciate.

Three of the architect's gambits seemed especially effective in this regard. The first was his talent for resonant juxtaposition. Scarpa's "staging" of sculpture, statuary, objects, and paintings—the ways they are discovered, mounted, framed, fore- and backgrounded, and, especially, combined—compels the viewer to perceive unexpected connections and layers of meaning. As well, Scarpa possessed a deep understanding of where the dynamic, "magnetized" moments lay in an architectural composition comprised of multiple periods and elements (some of them of his own making). Often he would place a significant artwork at such a point, so as to draw attention to it and bring the disparate parts into harmony. And there was Scarpa's strong sense of a building as a journey: The procession through a series of spaces, the experiences encountered along the route and their cumulative impact, was a defining aspect of his work.

Studying these and other of Scarpa's projects (notably his elegant, enigmatic Brion Cemetery near Treviso), taught me that, like

ABOVE: Museo di Castelvecchio in Verona, Italy, designed by Carlo Scarpa.
BELOW: I. M. Pei's Grand Louvre in Paris.

THIS PAGE: Diller Scofidio + Renfro's redesign of New York's Alice Tully Hall (TOP) broke open Pietro Belluschi's Brutalist original (LEFT).
OPPOSITE: A detail from the Gubbio Studiolo, completed in 1476 in Italy (TOP), and a cabinet in the 2002 Tanner Studiolo in Manhattan (BOTTOM).

a Fellini, an architect could employ a unique personal style to tell a universal tale—that a tectonic auteur, combining a strong sense of intention with a light touch, could lead one on a voyage that left a profound effect. Scarpa's oeuvre demonstrated that the language of architecture, which had been so difficult for me to parse, could be as meaningful, moving, and beautiful as any of the more legible storytelling arts. And because his method, at its most powerful, derived from the interplay of multiple states of time, the subject became one of my own presiding interests, setting me on a course that has arrived at this book.

Eventually, I came to appreciate another of Scarpa's signature qualities, that of creative fearlessness. If his work showed a profound knowledge of, and respect for, history, equally was the architect uninhibited in his manipulation of old buildings in the service of ideas. In fact, imagination and vision—rather than excessive caution or misguided historicism—have underlain some of the most memorable hybrid projects of our time. I. M. Pei's Grand Louvre, with its iconic glass pyramid, demonstrates how historic architecture can be revivified without a change of function, as does Renzo Piano's reconstruction of the earthquake-damaged California Academy of Sciences in San Francisco—a 410,000-square-foot cross-axial rectangle topped by a 2.5-acre green roof. In both instances, the architects made alterations to well-loved buildings that, while preserving much that existed, adjusted them to suit contemporary ideas about how such institutions might serve their constituencies.

It is also the case that changes to historic buildings don't have to be great architecture to have positive effects. Diller Scofidio + Renfro's renovation of New York's Alice Tully Hall, which sliced away a corner of Pietro Belluschi's bunker-like Brutalist theater and inserted an atrium, may be aesthetically dubious. But as Elizabeth Diller has pointed out, every architectural gesture was also an urbanistic one; the totality of the firm's alterations improved Tully's functionality and cracked open Lincoln Center's standoffish campus—a product of midcentury thinking about urban renewal—replacing its air of cultural elitism with a democratic, neighborhood-enlivening openness.

The Tully Hall project's focus on problem-solving, as opposed to statement-making, remains especially applicable to the hybridization of houses, for a simple reason: The great majority of residences were conceived of simply as shelter—not "architecture"—and this quotidian character makes them excellent candidates for creative reinterpretation.

One of my very favorite examples of this is the living room of the Tanner family apartment, in a typical prewar "classic six" on Man-

hattan's Upper West Side. In 1997, on a visit to the Metropolitan Museum of Art, Dr. and Mrs. Tanner—he is a successful practitioner, well-off by birth—saw the Gubbio Studiolo, the private study of Federico da Montefeltro, the Duke of Urbino. Completed in 1476, the studiolo's cabinets reveal, through partly open latticework doors, objects representing the duke's interests and history. What is remarkable is that the room is an illusion: a trompe l'oeil executed not in paint but in thousands of pieces of wood inlay.

Intrigued not only by the conception and execution but also by the idea of creating a shrine to one's own self-image, the Tanners decided to re-create the studiolo in their home, with a twist. They engaged a decorative artist to replicate the original as a trompe l'oeil painting—but filled the cabinets, not with the duke's objects, but rather reminders of their own life and family history, including a bowling ball, shoe polish, a corkscrew, and the family cat. The outcome was at once droll in the extreme and surprisingly provocative: an installation that set the Tanners' everyday existence in an art-historical context and connected the life and times of an Italian nobleman to the social, familial, and aesthetic preoccupations of modern-day, mid-level members of the American ruling class.

Of course, there are old/new residences far more "important" than the Tanner studiolo. But they often derive from the same impulse toward resonant self-expression. One of them, the London home of the Regency architect Sir John Soane, dates from

the late eighteenth and early nineteenth centuries and is today a world-famous house museum. The building, which he built and rebuilt as he tried out a dazzling range of ideas, is comprised of three adjoining townhouses that Soane combined over some thirty years and used as a residence, atelier, private art gallery, and ongoing design experiment. Soane's creation is utterly unique, yet in one respect it resembles many of the hybrid houses one sees today: The front remains traditional, while the rear explodes with the full force of modernity. Soane's "tradition," of course, is anything but: The domestic spaces reveal the singular nature of his work, and certain elements, notably the domed ceiling in the breakfast room, have been extensively sampled. But it is the back, where the architect broke through floors and walls to create stunning multistory spaces connected by colonnaded catwalks and winding stairs and atmospherically illuminated by a domed skylight, that has made the house's reputation. As well as abolishing the usual interplay of conventional rooms, the architect filled the zone with thousands of objects—antiquities, architectural fragments and models, statuary and busts, an incomparable assembly requiring (at least for this goggle-eyed visitor) multiple visits to take in. Yet despite the spectacle—the sense of bearing witness to greatness—the experience is surprisingly intimate. To enter Soane's house is to enter his talent, his obsessions, and, indeed, his soul. Few in the modern world would opt to live this way. Yet the place transforms one's thinking about what a modern—even a *modest* modern—house can be.

ABOVE LEFT: A gallery in the London home of Sir John Soane. ABOVE RIGHT: The Frank Gehry residence, Santa Monica, California.

In our own time, it would be difficult to find a residence more germane to the subject at hand than the Santa Monica home of architect Frank Gehry, which he created for his family in 1978. Like so many transformative ideas, the one underlying Gehry's project is so simple and inevitable as to seem, in retrospect, almost obvious. The architect purchased a pink, two-story Dutch Colonial bungalow built in 1920—as unassuming a place as could be imagined—and proceeded to wrap it in a riotous cornucopia of corrugated metal, chain link, glass, and wood, so that the outcome seems a kind of collision, as though an ordinary suburban home had been struck by a flying warehouse. The place resembles a collage, as much an artwork as an architectural statement, and its creator enjoyed the chaos. Told that there were ghosts in the house, Gehry wrote, "I decided they were ghosts of Cubism."

Much has been written about the project, by Gehry as well as others, and several observations bear repeating. The first is that, however intuitive the architect's gestures, his creation is not random, nor did he propose to sacrifice domestic pleasure on the altar of theory. "What Mr. Gehry is saying," wrote the critic Paul Goldberger, "is that there can be beauty in such harsh elements if they are carefully wrought and precisely put together, that they can create a new kind of order which can yield as much physical ease and comfort as a conventional house." It was also, observed the American Institute of Architects when it gave the place its 2012 Twenty-Five Year Award, "an authentic attempt to define the contemporary American suburban architectural condition." Indeed, the house is at once a nod to the industrial aesthetic of the region's midcentury modern residential design and, with its deadpan juxtaposition of an Ozzie-and-Harriet dwelling and a junkyard, a simultaneous embrace and rejection of suburbia in general and his own street in particular. Not least, Gehry's creation can be seen as crossing a line, an iconoclast's definitive acceptance of, and commitment to, his authentic nature. "I agonized about the symbols of the middle class to which I belonged, and to the particular symbols of my future neighbors," Gehry wrote. "I dug deep into my own history for cues and clues and followed my intuition."

As will be evident in the pages to come, the Gehry house has had a far-reaching impact—said the AIA, it "destigmatized the use of simple, raw, industrial materials for the bourgeois urban class." But style is beside the point. Like Soane's house, it is an act of creative investigation, a *cri de coeur*, and—like the Tanners' living room—a self-portrait. In taking something from the built world that spoke to him, and making of it what he would, Gehry said, *This is me.*

In selecting projects for this book, I looked for houses that were in one or another way personal expressions (or at any rate highly individual), and/or told architectural stories that might be perceivable by non-professionals. There are seven in the United Kingdom, the rest in the United States and Puerto Rico; though two received prizes from the Royal Institute of British Architects and one is a Los Angeles landmark, they were chosen not for their wow factor but for the ways in which their makers chose to respond to existing conditions (with one interesting exception). Thus the projects are meant to inspire rather than impress—or else to impress by providing inspiration—and reasonable people may disagree with the appropriateness of one or another choice. But if not all of the original structures would qualify for landmark status, and all of the interventions are not universally beloved, each shines a light through the prism of the subject in a singular way, demonstrating the multiple methods by which a hybrid home can enrich our personal lives and the worlds we inhabit.

And there is something else. I set out to write a book that was primarily "architectural" in character. But my background in film, and the fact that I am neither a scholar nor an intellectual, meant that I found myself attracted, over and again, to projects that not only conveyed a strong sense of narrative but whose architects and owners had great stories to tell. When I met the late architecture photographer Julius Shulman, whose home appears herein, he said there was little need for captioning in the volumes featuring his work because, as the man put it, "Nobody reads this stuff—they look at the pictures." Fair enough. But I hope you will make an exception in this case. If so, you'll discover that behind most great projects there are no less interesting tales to tell.

The London architect Shahriar Nasser has observed that an old building is like an old person: It has a lot to offer, if you treat it with respect, and listen to what it has to say. When you have the past to work with, you have a collaborator—but you have to divine its intentions. Iris Murdoch famously wrote that "love is the extremely difficult realization that something other than oneself is real"; as in human-to-human love affairs, when romancing an old house, the challenge is to try not to smother one's paramour with fantasies, expectations, and desires but to suppress one's ego and have the patience to discover what that house really is. As the eighteen projects that follow demonstrate, if you can follow Murdoch's dictum, and engage in a genuine dialogue with the past, that house will love you back. And the very personal hybrid of history and modernity you make together will grow more inspiring, supportive, and rewarding as the years pass.

1
CASA DELPIN
san juan, puerto rico

THE HOUSE OF CARLOS DELPIN AND HIS FAMILY occupies a narrow lot in the Miramar district of Santurce, the peninsula that forms San Juan's largest, most densely populated borough. "In the scale of the island, Santurce would be like Brooklyn," says architect Nataniel Fúster. "There are a lot of beautiful old houses, most of them from the late nineteenth century." The Delpin residence, however, is located in a newer extension of Miramar that is, in Fúster's formulation, "less nice. It's very crowded. The streetscape is not the best."

The original two-story, three-bedroom house, which dated from the 1940s, typified its era. A shallow front yard separated the structure from the sidewalk, and there was a deeper patio in the rear, with a structure at the lot's end that served as the maid's quarters. When he first toured the place, says Fúster, "the style was difficult to decipher. There were some Spanish Revival elements, like arches, and things that were very local, for example the use of colorful hydraulic tile. But also there were some midcentury modern lines, because the house was made from poured concrete. *And* someone had done a renovation and added Mexican Revival to the mix. So it was very strange." The interior Fúster describes as dark and densely partitioned. "The Delpins wanted larger, more open spaces—a place where they could relax and escape from city life," he recalls, a request complicated by the neighborhood's density.

The big idea, says Fúster, "was to create a dialogue between the old and the new by using the house's preexisting elements as inspiration." Principal among these was the lively concrete floor tiling the architect observed in the room abutting the front lawn, the stairwell, and the second-story spaces. "The pattern on the original tiles used rectangles," Fúster says. "We featured a very similar color palette, but

OPPOSITE: A small balcony adjoins the master suite in Casa Delpin. Architect Nataniel Fúster's double-height "vertical skylight" expands the interior space and modulates the strong Puerto Rican sun.

changed the design so that the shapes were more like rhomboids," producing a vibrant, Escher-like arrangement that the architect replicated in the perforations of the large-scale glass-reinforced concrete screen panels he used throughout the house. The outcome infused the entire experience with a very contemporary animation that still recalls the home's, and the district's, aesthetic traditions. This riff on history "synthesizes the design intentions," Fúster says—"bringing the old into the modern experience by reinterpreting the language."

Fúster's screens are in fact the design's most distinctive feature, and appear in three places. The first two serve as vertical double-height "skylights" on the upper front and rear elevations. Screen number three is horizontal in orientation and covers the lap pool in the new semi-enclosed living room, an architectural tour de force that is unquestionably the house's showpiece. Fúster crafted the space by enclosing the existing rear patio, a counterintuitive gesture that, though it eliminated the backyard, produced a grotto-like retreat from Miramar's density, in which the sensuality of water, ever-changing patterns of natural illumination, and the fresh air and precipitation coming through the screen's perforations (and a semi-enclosed patch of green on the room's other side) combine to very special effect. "A room like this works well in the tropics, because you don't have to close the house—you can have an intermediate, indoor/outdoor area," Fúster says. "It's amazing, because sometimes you have rain and sun at the same time, and the surface of the pool is dancing from the droplets coming in and also reflecting the light." Above all, the architect's screens set what otherwise would be a static object in motion. "The owners say it's like a light show that changes every day," he says.

ONE CASA DELPIN

17

OPPOSITE & ABOVE:

Fúster's inward-turning design, which forms a refuge from San Juan's density, incorporated an existing tree into the semi-enclosed living room. Fúster's screen design abstracts a pattern he discovered in the house's original floor tiles.

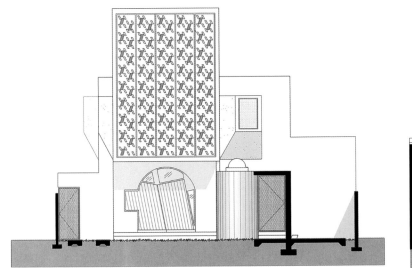

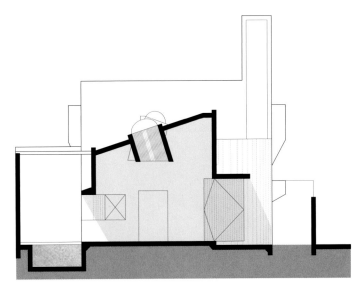

LEFT & OPPOSITE: The broader, street-facing screen covers a five-foot-wide balcony off of what was originally a second-floor family room but now belongs to the Delpins' child.

FOLLOWING SPREAD: The screen above the lap pool, which abuts the living room and terminates in a new dining area (formerly the garage), lets in sunlight and rain. Fúster based the down-projecting skylights on a design by Le Corbusier.

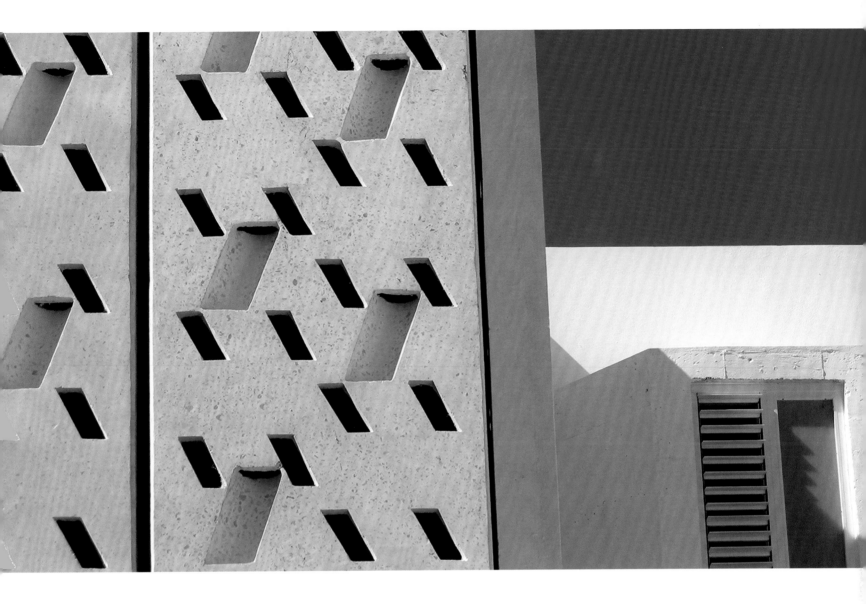

The need to balance the living room's natural light produced an arresting architectural quotation, a trio of angled, down-projecting cylindrical concrete skylights inspired, according to Fúster, by ones at Le Corbusier's 1960 Couvent Sainte-Marie de La Tourette outside Lyon. "One of the considerations of working with light in the tropics is that it's so strong that you need to offset it," the architect explains. "A lot of light comes in through the panels above the pool, and if we didn't balance it, you'd have strong illumination on one side and the rest of the room in deep shadow." The skylights correct the problem, and Fúster angled them to avoid having unmodulated rays pouring directly into the space. "Otherwise," he says, "you'd cook."

Light—and history—also influenced the design of the four second-floor windows that project outward from three sides of the house. "We were playing with the idea of depth," Fúster recalls. "In poured-concrete construction, the wall is very shallow. But if you look around Old San Juan, there is a lot of heavy Colonial construction, and the depth is very thick." The projecting windows, which resemble discreet sculptural fins on the exterior but read as angular concrete cones from within, "play with the eye and create the appearance of a thicker wall," the architect says. At the same time, Fúster lets us in on the trick, by cutting away the drywall around the apertures to expose the original shallow poured concrete. "The new construction is there, and so is the preexisting," he says. "It bounces the light and enriches the experience of the room."

Throughout design and construction, the relationship between past and present remained much on Fúster's mind. "In Puerto Rico, aspects of identity are very strong," he says. "We have a very interesting history—our present life with the U.S., and also the Spanish, African, and Indian heritage. I see architecture as a form of cultural expression, and so the way a building becomes informed by these aspects of identity makes it more interesting and layered." Even in ground-up projects, Fúster says, "There should be a dialogue, a connection to identity and history. It makes any building more profound—a richer experience."

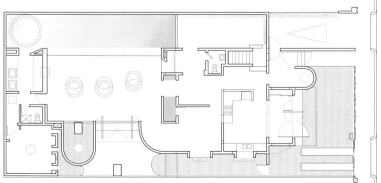

OPPOSITE: Fúster cut away the drywall around newly installed projecting windows, exposing the original poured-concrete walls.

ABOVE: The breakfast room/kitchen opens onto the newly enclosed street-front patio.

2
HUNSETT MILL
stalham, england

ONE OF THE MOST FREQUENTLY HEARD GEN-
eralizations about contemporary architecture is that it is
largely about form-making. This perception, moreover,
is usually pejorative: Given the popular preference for
tradition, the more outré (or merely unusual) a building
appears, the more it is seen to be an expression of its creator's ego, an arrogant refutation of history motivated by
nothing more than the desire to be novel (or noticed).

In truth, architectural forms are often reactive:
a response to existing conditions both architectural
and circumstantial (and, upon occasion, cultural), combined with
the demands of program. Hunsett Mill exemplifies this entirely.
Though striking, even whimsical, in appearance, and at first glance
a sly modern commentary on the impulse to sentimentalize the past,
the design, by the London firm Acme, is in virtually every particular
an imaginative, effective solution to a complicated set of problems.
Indeed, says Friedrich Ludewig, Acme's droll German-born principal, "there are very good reasons why people are not supposed to be
living here at all."

The house stands a few yards from the River Ant in England's historic Norfolk Broads. A protected landmark, the
Broads—a patchwork of shallow lakes and boat-friendly riv-
ers, and an abundance of flora and fauna—is a man-made wetland formed by centuries of unchecked peat cutting, "until they
had cut so much peat that the area flooded quite badly, and has
been half underwater ever since," Ludewig relates. "That was
about five hundred years ago—and with that began the never-
ending human struggle of how to get rid of all the water."

To create dry land for farming and grazing, numerous pumping
structures were erected across the Broads, and it is from one of these

OPPOSITE: The
original two-story late
eighteenth-century
cottage was home to a
mill keeper, his wife, and
their fourteen children.
The new extension,
clad in charred cedar,
reads as a shadow
behind the original.

that Hunsett Mill takes its name: a brick tower topped
by a windmill, with a diminutive, contemporaneous
mill-keeper's dwelling a few yards away, "a little hut
that was originally just one room upstairs and one
room downstairs," Ludewig says. "There is a stone set
into the mill dated 1666, though the building looks
like 1780 or maybe 1820. But there has been a mill in
that position for hundreds of years, because the problem is very old."

Around 1900, electricity replaced wind power and
eliminated the need for an overseer, at which point the cottage became
a private home. It was extended five times in the twentieth century, resulting in what Ludewig describes as "a weird concoction of spaces"—
small, low-ceilinged, shoddily constructed add-ons that maligned the
original cottage's simplicity, cut off the building from its surroundings,
and caused cracking and flooding as they settled into the soil.

Eventually the house was purchased by Ludewig's clients, two
couples with children who planned to use it as a weekend getaway
the families could jointly enjoy. Initially they proposed another
extension, with two bedrooms and a bath, to enlarge the existing
three-bedroom structure. But Ludewig observed that, while another add-on would provide additional space, it would not solve the
house's myriad problems, which included its bizarre disaffection
from the site. "You've got this amazingly beautiful countryside, next
to the biggest bird preserve in the UK," says Ludewig. "But you've got
this higgledy-piggledy house that is incredibly inward-looking, with
tiny windows, so that unless you went outside, you wouldn't see any
of the nature that was around you." The architect made his case, and
his clients agreed to remove all five of the twentieth-century interventions, restore the cottage to its historic appearance, and create a

single new volume that would answer the owners' programmatic requirements while maximizing the house's connection to the Broads.

Before design could begin, however, clients and architect had, like their predecessors, to contend with all that water. Unlike the earlier extensions, which were actually on lower ground than the cottage, the new construction would be elevated. But because the land surrounding Hunsett Mill is prone to flooding, Ludewig and his clients chose to address the larger issue of prevention, in partnership with the Environment Agency, the body tasked with the upkeep of the nation's flood defenses.

During the last century, the land around Hunsett Mill was protected by a seven-mile-long flood bank, running parallel to the Ant, that had badly deteriorated and was difficult, and expensive, to maintain—"because the wetland forests in the Broads have no roads, every time there was a breach, they would have to get on a barge with a crane, float down, and try to plug it," says the architect, "which was an absolute pain and a bit of a nightmare."

As an alternative, Ludewig's clients proposed that they buy a strip of land bordering the rear of the property from the neighboring farmer, and that the government abandon the existing flood defense and build a new, easily accessible one *behind* the house. "It's a sheet-piled wall with a clay bund, a bit more than two meters wide and sunk into the ground, with a new drainage channel beside it," Ludewig says. "And though it

ABOVE, OPPOSITE & FOLLOWING SPREAD: The cottage was awkwardly extended five times in the twentieth century. Rather than creating another add-on, architect Friedrich Ludewig replaced all of the additions with a discreet curving "tail" that, from certain angles, remains almost entirely invisible.

wasn't the cheapest thing in the world for the Environment Agency to build, it paid for itself quickly, because the seven miles of flood defense on the river was a problem they were glad to get rid of."

As for the house, Acme's design represents, in the firm's formulation, "a careful mediation between the requirements and aspiration of the client and the limitations of planning regulations." Though the original cottage had been compromised by the earlier extensions, it was still a historic building subject to rigorous preservation rules. "It had a size of about seventy meters square, and the mill-keeper and his family must not have been very tall, as one of the clients brushes his head against the ceiling every time he is inside," Ludewig says. "But we were only allowed twenty-three square meters more of floor space than the old extensions combined, and we were supposed to keep our project exactly the same height as the existing cottage roof." That meant setting two living rooms, five bedrooms, three baths, and a substantial kitchen into a total of roughly 220 square meters of space, capped by a low roof ridge.

From the outside, the new house seems to be smaller than it appears in photos. But the interior feels surprisingly light and capacious, in part because the mostly open-plan first floor is arranged around several double-height spaces, rising up above the kitchen, stair, main living room, and dining area—all interspersed with multiple picture windows—which combine with the undulating roof peaks and monolithic light wood finish to convey the scale and serenity of a country church. On the second floor, the five bedrooms and two principal baths are set along a catwalk that, with its views down to the first floor and up to the shaped ceilings, further encourages a sense of spaciousness.

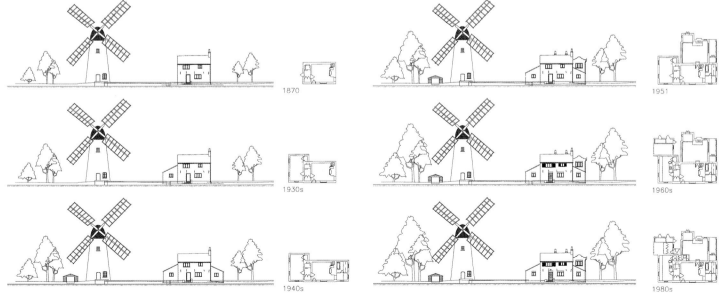

1870

1951

1930s

1960s

1940s

1980s

Yet the most distinctive quality of Acme's design is its discretion, embodied in a gesture that at once makes the new construction seem to disappear while also serving as the project's signature. The idea grew out of the mill's fame: In the same way that the leaning tower "represents" Pisa, Hunsett Mill, says Ludewig, "stands for the beauty of the Norfolk Broads." The postcard-ready view of the mill and cottage from the river appears in numerous sentimental artworks, atop chocolate boxes, and even as a jigsaw puzzle, a ubiquity that weighed on the architects during design development. "The planning law tells you how big you can be," says Ludewig. "What it doesn't tell you is how to deal with all the people who fell in love with the watercolors of how it used to be."

Acme's solution was to render the extension as a "shadow" of the cottage, a black volume that gently curves behind the original, following the line of the new flood defense to form a discreet architectural tail. Because of the angle, and the repetition of the old house's form and scale, the extension is from certain angles almost entirely invisible, only revealing itself gradually, and with a certain ambiguity, on approach. Ludewig narrates the experience: "When you come down the river, the first thing you see is the mill and the cottage, and it is all terribly innocent. And then you suddenly find there's a shadow, and then two shadows, and then suddenly there are three shadows." (In fact, on the extension's rear, there is an extra façade, formed by the need for an additional roof pitch to maintain the consistency of the gables' appearance as the house's outer elevation became elongated—"so in back there are four shadows," says Ludewig.)

The kink in the plan also served a domestic purpose, by giving the residents an outdoor seating area protected from sightseers' eyes. With its multiple waterways, the Broads remains extremely popular with boaters and, says Ludewig, "on a summer weekend there is a significant amount of traffic—some people who have maybe had a bit too much to drink and will wave and sound their horns." The concealed patio, invisible by boat on approach, keeps the outdoor experience private and peaceful.

The shadow concept was strengthened by Acme's use of charred cedar as cladding. A traditional method of timber preservation, with a centuries-long history of use in the region, lightly burning the exterior boards makes them naturally water- and bug-resistant and produces an appealing tactility, patinating a building's surface without erasing its material character. "Apart from making the extension more of a shadow, we thought, let's not try to 'out-brick' the original cottage, but to follow the Norfolk Broads's tradition of a utilitarian condition," Ludewig says.

To correct the preexisting building's visual isolation from its surroundings, the architects placed large, flush-mounted windows at strategic points on the façade, taking advantage of the course of the sun and the views while preserving the residents' privacy. "The land

toward the farmer's field in the back of the house is flat, so the views tend to be as wide as possible—you feel you can step out into the landscape," Ludewig says. Conversely, on the house's river-facing elevations, "there are ways to control how exposed you are—you don't want to feel you are part of a glass tableau." There are also multiple framed views of the mill itself, including an enormous double-height window that captures the entire, highly picturesque, tower. Ludewig acknowledges that the scramble of glazing appears eccentric from without. "But each of the windows serves a purpose and achieves certain things at different times of the day."

Interestingly, the project's method of construction, designed for maximal eco-friendliness and minimal site disturbance, also influenced the spatial character of the interior. The extension is, in effect, a prefab structure, according to Acme: "entirely made from solid cross-laminated timber walls, slabs, and roofs." This "exposed timber structure,"

ABOVE: The curving extension forms an exterior courtyard that conceals the residents from boaters passing on the River Ant. OPPOSITE: A highly reflective double-height window captures the image of the mill.

in the firm's formulation, "captures the essence of the geometry and materiality of the interior"—which means the folds and angles one sees on the exterior, the roofline in particular, appear within as well. "Which leads to interesting accidents," Ludewig says. By way of example, the architect points to the bedrooms, in several of which the low point of the roof falls in the middle, rather than at the edges. "The relationship of the roof to the walls is unusual. Yet we found that it creates a sense of spaciousness belying its diminutive size, and far exceeding the largest bedroom, where the high point is classically in the middle. So I wouldn't think of these rooms as awkward," Ludewig adds. "I would say the walls and roof are having a conversation that is not quite traditional."

"One could have added one more extension to the previous ones," says Ludewig, considering his firm's creation, "and dealt with the risks of flooding in other ways." Instead, Acme replaced a century's worth of piecemeal construction with "a harmonious intervention" that is "all but self-sufficient and has an actively positive effect on local ecology." In many respects, Hunsett Mill is a paradigmatic instance of form following function—a contemporary object that, while honoring the original, remains discreet, witty, and memorable.

ABOVE & OPPOSITE:
The seemingly random
scramble of windows
in fact captures
highly specific views.

Flush-mounted glass
preserves the object-
like nature of the new
construction.

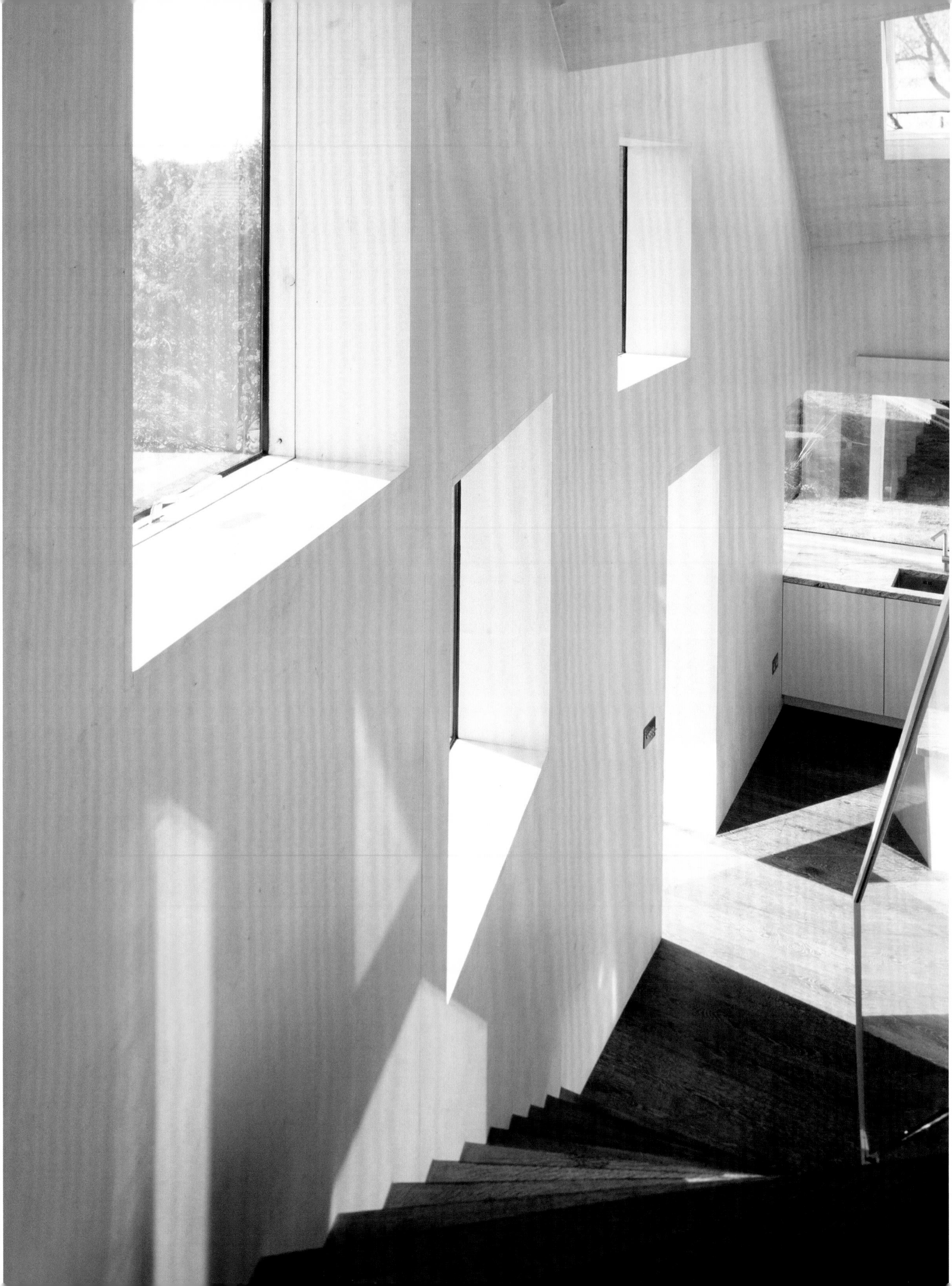

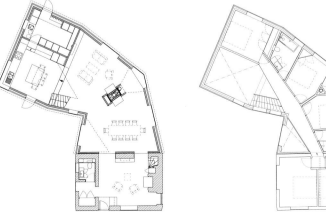

OPPOSITE & ABOVE:

An open-plan first-floor, multiple double-height spaces, abundant glazing, and a monolithic materiality make the extension feel larger and, in contrast to the original, less confining.

Of the ceiling, which follows the roof line, Ludewig says, "It's a debate we've had for a while—how much an external object should determine an internal one. Things that are not quite as you expect are often more exciting."

3

New York: Townhouses Revisited

SPLICED TOWNHOUSE

upper east side

+

LEEPER-BUENO HOUSE

harlem

THE CRITIC SHELLEY RICE, IN HER PROVOCATIVE study *Parisian Views*, hauntingly evokes the dislocating effects that the near-complete reconstruction of Paris in the nineteenth century had on its population. Thanks to what was perhaps the most audacious urban redevelopment project in history, the city was thoroughly modernized and made new. Yet for the citizens whose histories had been completely erased, what Rice describes as "the demolition of the collective personal and public mythologies inherent in city spaces" had, in a sense, deprived Paris of its future. "There was no transformation possible," Rice observes, "for in spite of all the hustle and bustle the city could no longer move in time—a movement that must go backward to go forward."

Though scarcely as extreme as it must have been in the Paris of Napoleon III and Baron Haussmann, this sense of being trapped in an eternal present can feel especially acute in modern-day New York—Manhattan in particular, where despite the presence of multiple protected historic districts, large swaths of the metropolis that might be considered essential have been cavalierly erased. Indeed, having myself lived in the city for nearly four decades, and borne witness to the remorseless extermination of its particularity and character by real estate interests (abetted by a succession of indifferent mayors), I can sympathize with the great nineteenth-century Parisian photographer Nadar, who said of his transformed environment, "I

OPPOSITE: In both townhouses, an innovative use of stairs lies at the heart of the architects' conception, bridging history and modernity as well as floors.

no longer know how to find myself in that which surrounds me."

Yet as these two Manhattan projects—both renovations of that most ubiquitous of New York typologies, the townhouse—remind us, market forces have been braided with the city's architecture for centuries, and factoring them into a contemporary design, rather than being malign, simply amounts to taking an inclusive view of history. Each project was undertaken by a young, somewhat iconoclastic New York office. Each uses a similar architectural gambit as its centerpiece. And though created for very different kinds of clients in neighborhoods that could not be less alike, each is in lively temporal motion: moving forward by invoking Rice's "collective personal and public mythologies," associations that create continuity with history and without which there can be no true progress—architectural or otherwise.

In fact, the townhouses that bring a stately elegance to many New York streets are, as the song goes, practiced at the art of deception. Outwardly they convey the privileged domesticity of the historic single-family residence. But behind the façades one typically finds a different reality: confining, nondescript apartments, carved out with brutal idiosyncrasy. The disconnect is especially startling in the exclusive environs of Manhattan's Upper East Side, where

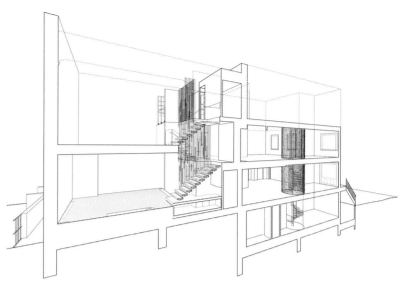

one assumes the good life still prevails—and where, in the course of two renovations over eight years, the architecture firm LTL Architects combined three different townhouse apartments into a twenty-first-century version of Old World grandeur.

"We always talk about how the constraints of a project drive the design solution," firm principal Marc Tsurumaki says of LTL's philosophy. "Here the constraints had everything to do with the typology of the New York townhouse." The structure, a four-story-plus-garden-level private residence, had been divided into apartments of different sizes and configurations. But there was an extra twist, in the form of a misalignment of floor levels between the house's two sides. While the street-front half retains the high ceilings and grand proportions of the original architecture, the garden-facing side features a greater number of floors with lower ceiling heights. Neither Tsurumaki nor partners David Lewis and Paul Lewis could determine how the house became divided against itself; their client speculates that when the building was converted to condominiums, the developers gutted the rear and compressed the ceiling heights to gain an extra floor. "But it's a typical New York story," Tsurumaki observes, "because what looks simple is actually the product of some complex, bewildering history of social and real estate negotiations that don't make any sense."

The misalignment didn't affect the initial renovation, which was confined to the townhouse's rear. LTL's client, who owned a small one-bedroom duplex spanning the below-street-level garden and first floor, purchased a second-floor studio apartment directly above his own residence and engaged the firm to refashion it into a master suite and connect it to the redesigned living/kitchen and guestroom/office levels below. This the architects accomplished with a spi-

LEFT, ABOVE & OPPOSITE: LTL Architects's scheme stitched together two apartments with a nearly thirty-foot-high, cascading grand stair.

ral staircase that forms the renovation's most distinctive element. Enclosed in a cylindrical blackened-steel screen featuring a perforated, laser-cut pattern—one that conveys a syncopated, Mondrianesque rhythm—the stair expresses the hermetic, inward-looking quality of the small, stacked spaces.

Despite the expansion, the triplex still "felt like a body without a head—it didn't have much public living space," the owner recalls; and when the first- and second-floor one-bedroom duplex facing the street became available, he purchased it. With their capacious original proportions, the duplex's two main spaces were to serve as grand living and dining rooms, while the intimately scaled triplex would contain the bedrooms and informal social areas. The front/rear misalignment, however, produced a daunting challenge: With a triplex in back and a duplex-plus-mezzanine in front, LTL was faced with combining six different levels, spread over three thousand square feet, into a coherent home.

The architects' solution amounted to a bravura example of vive la différence: They excavated a gap, measuring 3½ feet in width and rising up twenty-seven feet, between the front and rear apartments, thereby exposing five of the six floors to one another (the garden level remains out of view). "By revealing the condition, we created a ricochet of relationships between the different levels of the apartment," Tsurumaki says. The trio then sutured the apartments back together with an equally dramatic gesture: a grand public stair, partially enclosed by a slatted-oak-and-blackened-steel screen cascading down the five levels like a waterfall, that unites the floors and facilitates ever-changing, prismatic views as one travels up and down. Because the stair is both cantilevered and hung from the ceiling, it feels surprisingly weightless, a sensation intensified by the landings that float between the floor levels and make the entire residence seem airborne. The structure also helps unify the street and garden sides aesthetically: The screen plays off the pattern of the spiral stair's enclosure, converting its tight perforations into a more open, flowing visual music.

"It's not something you'd design from scratch," Tsurumaki admits. Yet crafting unity by exposing difference captures the character of New York overall—and the New York townhouse in particular. "The pleasure of working here is that you discover circumstances that follow no logic but are the product of unknowable historical processes that only occur in cities," the architect observes. "These idiosyncrasies are finally what fascinated us about the project—we tried not to paper over but to bring them into play and intensify them."

RIGHT: The top-floor living room (featuring a small mezzanine) overlooks the street and retains the townhouse's original architecture and proportions.

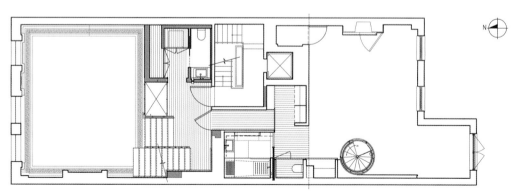

ABOVE & OPPOSITE: "It was very important that you could stand in the middle and see from the street to the garden," explains Marc Tsurumaki of the communicating front and back zones on the first floor.

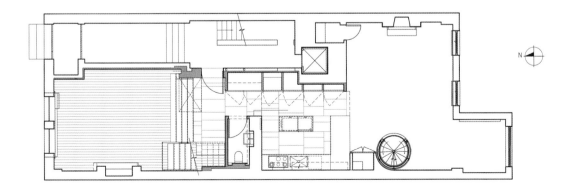

ABOVE & OPPOSITE:
Of the spiral stair
that spans the triplex,
Tsurumaki says, "We
wanted to define it as

a volume but not make
it heavy or obtrusive."
The pattern becomes
denser in the master

suite, where a sliding
glass panel within the
cylinder can be closed
for acoustic privacy.

LEFT & OPPOSITE: "To get into the house, we had to open a trap door and lower ourselves into the cellar," says architect Jonathan Knowles of his first site visit with partner Laura Briggs. The pair added a distinctive metal-clad bay to the traditional brick front, and a curtain wall of translucent panels in the rear.

WHEREAS THE HISTORIC TRAJECTORY OF LTL'S PROJECT ultimately remained a mystery, the saga of this turn-of-the-last-century row house, on the other side of Manhattan in Harlem, was all too familiar to its owners. "My father loved the area, and he was exuberant about this property," says Yvette Leeper-Bueno, who lives there with her husband and two children. Today the residence, half a block from Morningside Park and with a sublime, above-the-treetops view of the Cathedral of St. John the Divine, stands on a stretch of W. 112th Street notable for its calm and consistency. But in 1982, when Franklin Leeper bought the place, the area was infested with crime, and the house itself—chopped up into tiny, single-room occupancy residences—was inhabited by drug dealers and hard-luck cases. Even so, Leeper-Bueno recalls, "My father liked this street, and the fact that it had the first row of townhouses as you set foot into Harlem's west side"; he also appreciated its proximity to two green spaces (Central Park is a few blocks to the southeast). With dreams of a better tomorrow, he took it on.

Ten years later, Franklin walked away. "He was calling the police constantly, he couldn't collect rent, he couldn't deal with the woes of the people," Leeper-Bueno explains. In the ensuing decade, the violations and back taxes piled up, the structure deteriorated as pipes burst and fires were set—and then the heavens delivered the coup de grâce: During a violent storm, the façade was struck by lighting and partially collapsed.

Yet dreams die hard, which was why Adrian Bueno, Leeper-Bueno's husband, found himself before a building he describes as "a complete shambles," listening to a proposition. "Frank was asking me, 'Why don't you get involved?'" recalls Bueno. "And I was thinking, this is the Wild West." But the couple had their own dream of home ownership. And, Leeper-Bueno admits, "There was the sentimental value. My family had history here." So, as Franklin had done a generation earlier, they took the plunge.

The first challenge—apart from buying the house's freedom from various city agencies, a bureaucratic and legal nightmare that consumed hundreds of thousands of dollars—was finding an architect brave enough to go into the place. "It was completely collapsed," says Jonathan Knowles of Briggs Knowles Architects, recalling his first visit. Still, Knowles and partner Laura Briggs were intrigued by what she calls the "space puzzle" of creating an owner's triplex apartment (including a new rooftop penthouse) and two rental apartments on an ultra-tight sixteen-foot-wide lot, and the challenge of improving the house's quality and efficiency. They also responded to the owners'

enthusiasm for a rich and varied experience within the overall space. "I said to Jonathan, 'I don't care if I like it or not—I want it to be about something,'" Bueno recalls. In fact, the house is about many things, among them light, material, geometry, and perception. Above all, the couple's triplex presents a complex spatial narrative—as full of startling mood changes as the neighborhood itself.

This is particularly evident in the house's most arresting new feature. To compensate for the narrowness of the lot, the architects relocated the stair from the side to the rear, making a twenty-eight-foot-high shaft in which they hung a plate-steel stair to create a sense of buoyancy, widening the landing between the second and third floors into a floating mezzanine that effectively turns the entire construction into a habitable space. This Briggs and Knowles capped with an equally bravura gesture: the replacement of the rear brick elevation with a curtain wall of translucent panels, into which they inserted glass panes that reveal views of the outdoors.

Equally dynamic is the building's façade. "We were very conscious of making sure that the outside extended

OPPOSITE & ABOVE:
The architects removed the original side stair and replaced it with a 28-foot-high plate steel construction in back, to widen the narrow rooms.

into the house," Briggs says. Toward this end, the architects designed a two-story, galvanized steel–clad bay window that angles toward Morningside Park. Apart from drawing in light and views, the window's perceptual legerdemain vitalizes the streetscape: From one end of the block, only a narrow plane of apparently freestanding metal can be seen. Observed from the park, however, the window appears to be directly "looking at" the viewer and physically reaching out to the neighborhood.

Briggs and Knowles acknowledge that the architecture's interleaving of past and present, at once piquant and oddly haunting, has much to do with their clients' aspirations. "They're contributing to the neighborhood as individuals," Briggs says, "partially because Yvette has a relationship to the property that's an old one, but also because they're not holding on to what it used to be." By responding to the family's desires with an aggressively forward-looking design that nonetheless seems to breathe in all of Harlem's complexity, the architects transcended both gentrification and preservation, to produce an urban residential template for the future—not what Shelley Rice describes as "a *this is* severed from its *this has been*," but rather a *this will be*.

ABOVE: The new bay window is tilted slightly, to give the living room, and a child's room directly above it, a view of Morningside Park, nearby at the corner.

ABOVE: The spatial fluidity in the top-floor master suite includes a translucent sliding door that exposes the hot tub to the bedroom.

LEFT: Briggs and Knowles relocated the old stair to maximize the house's width.

4

ASTLEY CASTLE
nuneaton, england

IN HIS BOOK *MONUMENT BUILDERS*, THE ENGLISH author Edwin Heathcote observes that the Arcadian landscape garden decorated with classical ruins and remembrances "has become an archetype of the burial ground" and traces its origins to Jean-Jacques Rousseau, who famously envisioned Man as a noble savage in a self-created Eden, a paradise made poignant by the inevitability of loss. In the eighteenth century, Rousseau's influence dovetailed with the new study of archaeology and the fashion for the romantic garden to produce idealized landscapes in which fragments and monuments served as *memento mori*—reminders of one's mortality.

At first sight—viewed from the gate opening onto the greensward that surrounds it—Astley Castle, outside the English village of Nuneaton, perfectly fits the profile: It is, says architect Freddie Phillipson of the London firm Witherford Watson Mann, which executed the castle's resurrection, "a grand ruin in the picturesque tradition, isolated in the landscape." The closer you get, the more this first impression dissipates. For one, there is the realization that, within the jagged remains of the old southern elevation, the first that you see, a rectilinear wall of new brick has been inserted. But it's not until you pass through one of the three openings that comprise the entrance, into a double forecourt completely open to the sky, that you realize how completely Astley contravenes the garden ruin's classical representation of death—because one is everywhere surrounded by life's palpability: woodsy aromas, sunlight and breezes, birdsongs. With a directness as startling as it is pleasurable, the centuries-old structure locates you in the moment.

That the present dominates so strongly is remarkable, as the castle has been a functioning dwelling (based on the best reckoning) since

OPPOSITE: While the castle's historic front façade, at right, remains largely intact, the side view reveals Witherford Watson Mann's contemporary intervention. The use of masonry—stone and brick—connects old and new.

the thirteenth century. According to a history compiled by the Landmark Trust, the structure's current custodians, Astley began as "a fortified manor house, crenellated and moated in 1266," around the end of the high medieval period. As the centuries passed, the castle grew in reputation as well as size, becoming known as "the home of three queens of England"—Elizabeth Woodville, Elizabeth of York, and Lady Jane Grey. After it passed from the Grey family in 1600, the structure got bigger but not, according to the Trust, better. After the mid–seventeenth century, Astley changed hands several times and "was never a significant main residence, but always half forgotten." Converted into a hotel after World War II, the castle was rendered uninhabitable by a fire in 1978, after which it became progressively more unstable, overgrown, and near to collapse.

The UK's Landmark Trust, which characterizes itself as "a building preservation charity that rescues historic buildings at risk and gives them a new future by offering them for holidays," got interested in saving Astley in the mid-1990s but was unable to make it work until 2005 when, according to the Trust, "it was accepted . . . that conventional restoration was no longer achievable," and "parts of the castle had . . . to be taken down." This transformation in perception was crucial. Quite apart from the expense, "the idea of restoration was problematic," says Phillipson. "Conceptually it was very difficult to pinpoint a single entity for Astley, which has been continuously adapted since the Norman period—so what do you restore it to? Do you go back to 1500, or 1700?"

In 2007, to sort out the double challenge—of finalizing and stabilizing the ruin and creating holiday accommodations for up to eight vacationers—the Trust held an architectural competition.

There were a dozen entries, and a look at the schemes developed by the practices is fascinating—a kind of tour of contemporary thinking about adaptive reuse and the relationship between old and new. Though several of the competing firms proposed occupying the ruin with architecture that clearly distinguished itself from the original—one used the castle as a sheath for a glass volume, another featured a dramatic vaulted roof—"most of the firms proposed to stabilize the ruin, so that it became a sort of landscape museum, and then set a habitable house to one side," Phillipson observes.

WWM's winning proposal took a different tack. Rather than separating the two, says the architect, "our strategy was that the new architecture would both stabilize the ruin *and* provide the accommodation in one move." This was partly pragmatic, partly philosophical. The firm did considerable research into the surrounding landscape, which was dotted with historic elements, in-

ABOVE: On the castle's rear elevation, where the walls were largely intact, WWM set the glazing at different depths. "That maintains the appearance of a ruin—the windows are voids," notes project architect Freddie Phillipson.

cluding the moat, a fish pond, and a medieval church just to Astley's south; the presence of a larger, layered history inspired the architects to view their contribution as part of the continuing occupation of the site. "The accommodation we were being asked to provide was too small to fill the footprint of the expanded castle," Phillipson explains. "Therefore what we proposed was to occupy the oldest territory—the medieval keep—and leave the rest as stabilized but open to the sky in the form of outdoor courts."

The first challenge for the team (which at different points included firm principals Stephen Witherford, Christopher Watson, and William Mann) was simply figuring out what, precisely, they had on their hands. "The site was completely overgrown, and full of twenty-five lorry loads of rubble," Phillipson recalls. "So we really didn't know what it was until after it had been cleaned out and pinned together." Parts of the castle were too fragile to stabilize and were taken down, nota-

LEFT & OPPOSITE:
"As the roof went, the walls became vulnerable to the weather, and started delaminating," Phillipson explains. WWM's scheme created a contemporary relevance that evolved organically from the castle's history while also stabilizing it.

bly the Victorian-era extension at the building's north and a half-timbered section, both heavily compromised by the fire. WWM's design evolved as the site clearing continued and more knowledge regarding Astley's content came to light. "For example, the two courtyards were originally drawn as one," Phillipson says of the pair of roofless enclosed spaces, separated by a wall fragment with fireplaces on both sides, that lies behind the castle's iconic entry façade. "We didn't know about the significance of the fireplace stack until the clearing had happened, and the building historian was able to determine that it was crucial to the story of the castle's development." The court beyond the trio of entry doors, it transpired, belonged to a fifteenth-century "high status chamber," whereas the other great room dated from 1627—thus the two hearths. "What began as a single entity became one of the most complex spaces to resolve," Phillipson says.

The stabilization of the original took eighteen months and was completed prior to the start of new construction. The historic walls proved to be substantial, nearly six feet in thickness and with rubble infill between exposed stacked stone. To shore them up, cores were drilled through the walls and anchors inserted, followed by injections of a "cementitious mix." "That pinning together enabled the walls to hold up the new masonry we were going to add."

In fact, the interdependence of old and new is what gives the entirety its stability. "The principle was that the new construction would be built off the old walls," Phillipson explains. The architects designed what he describes as "this very irregular spider" comprised of brick walls and piers and reinforced concrete lintels, which they inserted into the historic masonry shell; the brickwork filled in the gaps in the old walls, enclosing the spaces, but followed the irregular lines of the original masonry so that the difference between the past and present remains distinct and legible. All of the new construction apart from the original plan—including the various roof elements, interior walls, and window frames—was executed in wood, which introduced warmth, craft, and an aspect of domesticity to the revitalized structure.

Part of the pleasure of Astley's design derives from the meticulousness with which the elements were detailed, the brickwork in particular. To achieve the tightest possible connection where old and new masonry meet, the architects selected a "D36" brick from the Danish company Petersen, the narrowness of which enabled a tighter joint with less mortar. WWM also wanted the brick to meet the undulating edges of the ruin,

rather than to slip behind it, "and we had very specific rules about that," Phillipson says. "We wanted no less than two-thirds of a cut brick exposed, rather than a lot of little pieces." The team was no less particular regarding the glazing. "That was another principle: We would not make any new openings in the existing walls—we'd use the gaps that accident had provided." This opportunism remains most evident in the V-shaped gash in the so-called spine wall separating the open courts from the interior. "At the upper level, there's a bigger opening so we were able to insert large windows with views from the upstairs dining area across the courtyards and out to the landscape," Phillipson says.

As for the living spaces, "once it was decided that the accommodations would go back in the oldest part of the castle, the question was how to arrange it," Phillipson recalls. "At the competition stage, we established what William [Mann] calls an upside-down house, with the bedrooms below and the living areas upstairs." The decision enabled WWM to create a single, grandly proportioned living/dining/kitchen hall, some fifteen feet high, which captures the entirety of the castle's founding proportions and opens up views of the surrounding landscape.

From the first, two ideas influenced the new architecture's character. "One of the principles was to use the wood elements to create comfort in what is otherwise quite an austere shell," Phillipson explains—"the masonry stabilizes the castle, and the carpentry provides the conditions for habitation." The other idea involved the fact that guests would be, in effect, occupying a ruin. "Therefore a sense of incompleteness should be perceivable everywhere, including all of the new rooms. Each has three ingredients from the overall scheme: the stabilized fabric, some new masonry, and some carpentry. Nothing is a single entity that's been executed in one way, which creates a slightly restless quality."

Most impressively, the new architecture brings out the spatial pleasures of the ruin by suggesting how slender the line is between the open and the enclosed. This culminates in the central stair, which connects the two levels, a construction with not too much of anything, but just enough of everything. "The stair is an emblem of what's happening more broadly in the scheme because we took away as much as we could—if you take away more, it just becomes an object, and if you added more, you'd have a box," Phillipson observes. "The stair is about scaling your experience in space—how you take

a grand ruin, introduce comfort, and eventually something quite intimate, which is the thing that you touch."

The slim line between open and enclosed reflects a larger theme of the castle's reconstruction: the presence of the past in the moment, and the contribution of those enjoying it to the site's continuum. This is embedded in the reality of the building, in which historic and contemporary narratives intermingle. "We built into what was already a layered topography," says Phillipson, and the conversion of that topography into a palpable, even theatrical, narrative is one of the plan's great strengths. Preserving the first two rooms as open forecourts, a transitional zone between landscape and structure, launches a "stepping out of your everyday routine into another version of the world," says the architect—"a picturesque ruin wherein the idea that all things must pass is really palpable, but at the same time you have a sense of vitality and pleasure. Leaving everything open in front really supports that: the idea that the moment you step through the façade wall, you're enacting a heightened version of everyday life."

The firm's project notes reference the artist Gordon Matta-Clark, who famously made huge slices through abandoned vernacular structures, exposing their rooms to one another, and revealing simultaneous states of time. "Here it was accident that achieved what Matta-Clark had done deliberately," says Phillipson, which the architects turned to the advantage of the castle's program. "We were trying to draw on Astley's ruined fabric as a setting for the events people celebrate in these holiday houses, mostly birthdays and anniversaries. They're taking stock of time, and we saw the accumulated time of the ruin as being a setting for these events." This culminates in the dining area—"a moment where the thirteenth, fifteenth, seventeenth, and twenty-first centuries all come together for the setting of the meal."

At the end of our discussion, Phillipson makes an observation about the project that pertains to much architecture that hybridizes old and new. "You can't understand the whole thing in one go," he says. "You put together what the architecture is trying to do by moving around it. There's an older narrative that's just the facts of the building. But how you choose to knit it all together is ultimately the story you're writing for the building—the true narrative." And as with all good stories, what is concealed and left to the imaginations of the inhabitants is just as important as what is shown. "You're working up to something that's incomplete," the architect says. "And what we're making is itself unfinished. It's not deterministic—it leaves itself open to future adaptation."

Perhaps ironically, the ultimate success of WWM's scheme for Astley Castle lies in its resistance to "making architecture": rather

than standing apart, the firm's design emerges from the original. "A lot of what you see at first glance is the extraordinary character of the walls, the brutal discontinuity of history," Phillipson says. "Only then are you welcomed into spaces that are comfortable enough to inhabit. William has a very good phrase about 'not keeping history at arm's length,' and there isn't an arbitrary separation between *then* and *now*. This is just another phase of the occupation of something that's been evolving for eight hundred years."

OPPOSITE & ABOVE: One of two adjoining open courts that sit behind the main façade and produce a highly theatrical experience that bridges interior and exterior space.

PRECEDING SPREAD:
The expansive second-floor window above the front door bridges the living and dining areas and overlooks the open courts below.

OPPOSITE & ABOVE:
The soaring open courts give way, on the first floor, to a series of discreet, enveloping spaces that establish a domestic character. WWM used multiple masonry elements, including stone, tile, and brick—"tonally quite similar, so the transitions seem easy and seamless," says Phillipson.

FOLLOWING SPREAD:
Reversing the usual order, WWM set the living, dining, and kitchen zones on the second floor, in a single great room, to take advantage of natural light and views.

PRECEDING SPREAD:
The galley kitchen
abstracts a medieval
cooking fireplace.

OPPOSITE & ABOVE:
The cozy first-floor
bedrooms receive an
infusion of warmth from
timber elements.

5

TEN BROECK COTTAGE
livingston, new york

OPPOSITE: Brian Messana and Toby O'Rorke's country home unites a Colonial farmhouse and a new CorTen-clad addition.

THE NEW YORK-BASED ARCHITECTS BRIAN Messana and Toby O'Rorke first discovered what would become their country home in rural Columbia County, a few hours north of the city, in 2001. Both men were drawn to the property immediately. Though the house sat at the exposed intersection of two roads, it came with just over eight acres of land, the centerpiece of which was a 1,600-tree apple orchard. "And it had a lot of sky," O'Rorke recalls. "A lot of country places are stuck in the woods, but this was really airy."

There were two structures on the acreage: a somewhat derelict farmhouse and a concrete shed. The former dated from the Colonial era but had been altered repeatedly, and the iteration the architects found was finalized, they estimated, in the mid-1800s. "It hadn't really been messed with in the twentieth century, other than the addition of a metal roof that kept it standing," O'Rorke relates. "But the house was abandoned in the 1960s, when the property became a camp for seasonal apple pickers—you weren't allowed to put migrant workers in wood structures, so they built the concrete shed as a dormitory."

For architects, part of the pleasure of investigating an old structure lies in deciphering its narrative, and the farmhouse did not disappoint. A Dutch "H-bent" frame building made from massive hand-hewn timbers, "the house was built by the Ten Broecks, one of the original settler families of the area," says O'Rorke. "The earliest date we could find was 1734, but they obviously got here earlier than that." Initially, the family would have lived, in effect, in a hole. "They claimed their piece of land, excavated the basement, lined it with stone, and roofed it, then lived below ground until they could afford to go up. We don't really use it, but it's one of my favorite places in the house," says O'Rorke of the subterranean space, indicating an original wattle-and-daub wall. "There's a nice old leather strap that would have been part of a door hinge, and you can see the wall where the fireplace went." The story grew harder to follow as the architects removed partitions and extrusions and stripped the structure to its frame, simply because so much had been done to the place.

"The windows had moved all over, entrances and exits had been changed; we found a door that led to a stair that was no longer there," says O'Rorke. "There was no way of guessing what the original thing looked like."

Messana O'Rorke is known for work in the modernist mode—well-planned, unadorned rectilinear spaces that, despite moments of material richness, border on the severe—and so it comes as no surprise that the architects' original plan was to live in the concrete shed. "That excited us more than the old, tumble-down thing," O'Rorke admits. They spent summers there (the shed was unwinterized), "and it was fantastic: You opened all the doors, the dogs ran in and out, and you just occupied the space," he recalls. "It was like being in a loft." Though the architects originally planned to first renovate the shed, they eventually realized they'd have to begin with the house—in part because the shed was habitable, but also, O'Rorke recalls, "because the house began to intrigue us more. We were just sitting in the shed all the time, looking out at it and thinking about it."

The partners' initial plan involved adding an extension that was stylistically compatible with the original. "We felt we should be respectful of the 1734 building," O'Rorke explains. "We drew up this whole set of plans, and then we looked at them and thought, *Why are we doing this?* It looked like crap, and it wasn't really honoring the house anyway—it was pastiche-ing." Taking a step back, Messana and O'Rorke reconsidered the Colonial architecture and realized they felt a kinship to it. "We really relish the simple, and that's exactly how the Colonialists were. Everything about their life was simple; they didn't have a lot of stuff—they would burn down houses just to retrieve the nails—and the buildings they designed were stark and straightforward and practical. They were the early American modernists."

Accordingly, the architects decided that an extension designed in their signature style would pay homage to the original more genuinely than something faux Colonial. Casting about for inspiration, Messana and O'Rorke took note of the local custom of parking metal trailers next to traditional wooden houses. "That's the way a lot of people choose to expand up here," says O'Rorke. "You also see a lot of industrial debris, rusty things. The river"—Taghkanic Creek, a short walk from the house—"is full of it." Thus the pair chose to append an architectural extrapolation of a trailer form to the back of the old house, and to clad it in a CorTen steel that would rust into a color in sympathy, not only with metal refuse, but the rural landscape.

Rather than posing a problem, the old house's dilapidation proved advantageous. "There was nothing of value internally, so we didn't have to deal with anything that was aesthetically an obstacle," O'Rorke says. "We were left with the form and structure, which were beautiful." The architects stripped the H-bent frame of paint almost entirely—"we decided we liked the look, with old bits of wallpaper stuck in it, so we only went so far." They also benefited from serendipity. Some of the original wide-plank white pine floor remained, but not on the ground level, where it had been entirely replaced by plywood. "We went into town to see if the architectural salvage shop had any eighteenth-century flooring, and the guy told us no," O'Rorke recalls. "Then he rang a few days later to say that someone had shown up with

BELOW: The house when the architects discovered it. The nearby concrete shed was built to house seasonal apple-pickers. OPPOSITE: A below-grade door leads to an exercise room.

a truckload of it that he'd been storing in a shed since he demolished a Colonial house in the 1970s—he just happened to come to town the week we were looking, and it fit into our house perfectly."

The architects used the house's sole surviving six-over-six sash window as a template for the others and clad the structure in cedar siding and shakes, producing what O'Rorke describes as "the perfect Monopoly house." The simplicity continues within, where a new wall with a double-sided fireplace lightly separates the living and dining areas below, and the upstairs features a pair of small bedrooms with shaped ceilings and a bath between them.

In contrast to the Colonial building, with its small windows and inward-looking flavor, Messana and O'Rorke's new wing—featuring a kitchen, storage, and a bedroom and shower on the main floor and an exercise space, steam room, and sauna in the cellar—is light-washed and open to the landscape. A twelve-inch-wide glass gasket separates the old and new volumes, and the addition is slightly raised above ground level, so that the entirety appears—despite the muscular steel cladding—to float. The garden-facing wall is composed entirely of full-height sliding glass doors, and the cellar space receives daylight from a large glass door and a row of skylights.

When asked for advice on combining the historic and contemporary, O'Rorke's response proves as no-frills as the home he and Messana created. "It all comes out of what you see when you see the old—there isn't a set solution," the architect says. "It draws on what your program will be, what you're looking for, and especially what exists." Like the Ten Broecks, who began by digging a hole, "You work with what you have."

PRECEDING SPREAD:
The addition opens
completely to the
landscape via a series
of sliding glass doors.

ABOVE: A narrow
glass channel
separates old and new.
OPPOSITE: The stair
in the farmhouse,
beside the portal to
the addition, leads
to the second-floor
bedrooms.

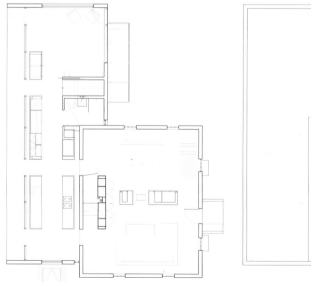
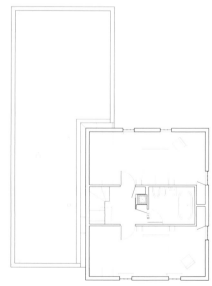

ABOVE & OPPOSITE:

On the farmhouse's first floor, a new wall, with a double-sided fireplace, lightly divides the living and dining spaces. The architects made the dining table from flitch-sawn boards and saw horses.

OPPOSITE & BELOW:
The addition features
the kitchen at one end
and a bedroom and
shower at the other, with
storage in the middle.

RIGHT: The cellar-level exercise room draws natural illumination from skylights on the front of the addition.
OPPOSITE: The farmhouse bedrooms received monochrome treatments that highlight the volumetric simplicity of the building's character.

6

GREENWICH HOUSE
greenwich, connecticut

OPPOSITE: Architect
Allan Greenberg
appended a quiet
two-story Miesian
glass box to an
extravagant classical
revival confection in
Connecticut.

IN THE UNITED STATES, THE NAME ALLAN Greenberg remains strongly associated with contemporary classical architecture, in particular the residential variant, though his firm has worked extensively on college campuses, and his commercial and institutional projects include the Treaty Room at the Department of State. "From 1972 until the mid-1980s I was the only person in this country doing this work," observes the soft-spoken South Africa–born architect. What's more, "Because I'm an immigrant, my major focus is on American buildings—when I travel, I don't go to Europe. I stay in the U.S."

Thus it is surprising to discover not only how much Greenberg knows about international modernism, but how much he appreciates it—"unlike my fellow classicists." Of course, the architect's heroes, notably Alvar Aalto, Le Corbusier, and especially Mies van der Rohe, whose Barcelona pavilion he particularly admires, came out of the classical tradition. "In every office he ever had, Mies hung a drawing of an Ionic column—he took it everywhere with him, from Germany to the U.S.," Greenberg relates.

Greenberg's affection for the "classical modernists," as he calls them, is braided with his distaste for the balkanization of history and the present. This is evident in what he calls "my major commitment to contextualism, something that differentiates me from younger classical architects." Contextualism, in fact, has often been a Trojan horse for maintaining the status quo, as when adventurous contemporary designs are rejected by developers—or even those overseeing historic districts—because they don't imitate the design language of their surroundings. Greenberg, however, defines it differently: "Good contextualism," he believes, "means that each building should exemplify what it is you'd like to see next door."

Asked for an example, Greenberg immediately cites the 1965 Chicago Civic Center (now the Richard J. Daley Center), "designed by Jacques Brownson, a student of Mies, and one of the greatest postwar buildings in the U.S., I believe." After describing in detail the particular character of the structure's columns and windows, Greenberg notes the Daley Center's close proximity to Holabird & Roche's 1911 City Hall, a classical revival landmark distinguished by majestic colonnaded façades. Of the surprisingly sympathetic and dynamic interplay between the two very different masterworks, he says, "It's one of the few times when an architect was able to create a modern building and relate it to a classical structure next door—very unusual and powerful."

Greenberg might have had Chicago in mind when he undertook the renovation and expansion of this nineteenth-century wedding cake of a house in Greenwich, Connecticut. The structure, a classical revival mansion girdled by two levels of terracing and large (and larger) Doric columns, is highly theatrical; the outsized front steps, which taper gradually as they ascend to the porch, seem specifically designed for making grand exits and entrances. "Its exuberance transcends its architectural limitations," says Greenberg, accurately and not unkindly.

"Apart from fixing up the house, which was in terrible shape, they had in mind an extension with a two-story living room with big glass windows, but divided up into little panes," Greenberg recalls of the residents. His initial scheme was more in sympathy with the existing house—"classical meets Arts and Crafts," the architect explains. "One day I was sitting with my client, and I said, 'You know, painting the dividers of every one of those windows will be hugely expensive—maybe we should just do a steel-and-glass pavilion, like Mies's Farnsworth House.' And she immediately said, 'Yes—let's do it!'"

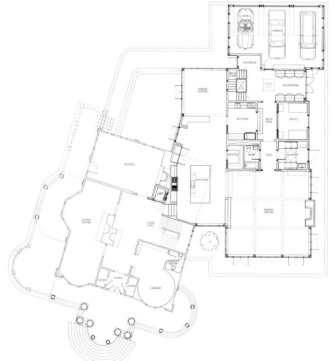

Greenberg did indeed have the owners' interest in mind. "But," he admits, "I also wanted to get my Mies on."

In the existing house, Greenberg consolidated rooms on both the main and second floors to produce a more graciously scaled formal living room and four substantial suites for the couple's children upstairs. "My clients were very conscious of wanting to make the best use of the space the house had to offer, and not trying to force the plan," he says. The new pavilion, which connects to the earlier structure by a short flight of stairs, includes a sun-filled, high-ceilinged family room, spacious open kitchen and breakfast room, and various support spaces on the ground level, and an expansive master suite above. (There is also a squash court in the basement.) "I didn't want to compete with the exuberance of the original," Greenberg explains. "I wanted mine to be a kind of lateral extension that goes off to one side."

While the old and new components remain distinct from one another, Greenberg united them—like Brownson in Chicago,

but more explicitly and deliberately—via the use of columns. "The Doric ones on the original have a very tactile presence and organize everything, and I tried to infuse my columns with the same life and presence—there's a magic about an I-beam, and you see all the nuts and bolts." Additionally, "I tried to take all the horizontal lines of the old house and relate them to the floor heights of the new wing," Greenberg recalls. His original plan in fact specified narrow metal terraces that echoed those on the old house, but they were ultimately eliminated and, considering the harmonious outcome, would surely have been a distraction. Instead, each building sustains an independent personality yet together form a credibly coherent object, its parts united by a shared classical DNA.

"I've always prided myself on being able to do anything," Greenberg says, "and I was glad to be able to show what an architect like myself can do

ABOVE & OPPOSITE: Greenberg envisioned a sympathetic relation- ship between the two structures' vertical and horizontal elements, similar to the interplay between Chicago's Richard J. Daley Center and City Hall.

with steel and glass." Yet though the house and pavilion harmonize on the exterior, the life within remains divided, in a way that expresses the difference between the way families lived in the past and our contemporary preferences. "We almost never come in here," the owner admits, showing me the tastefully decorated formal living and dining rooms in the old house. "We live in the addition." This is a function not only of the modern penchant for hanging out in intercommunicating casual spaces like family and breakfast rooms and kitchens, but for the pleasures of sunlight, views, and natural ventilation—benefits typically associated with modernism. In the house in Greenwich, the irony of Greenberg's contextualism lies in the way it demonstrates that the present and past often partner more comfortably in architecture than everyday life.

OPPOSITE & ABOVE:
In the original house,
Greenberg combined
two spaces on the first
floor to create a formal
living room that is at

once traditional and
loft-like, a complement
to the fully glazed, high-
ceilinged family room in
the new wing.

7

COB CORNER
ermington, england

ERMINGTON, IN THE SOUTHWESTERN COUNTY of Devon—the South Hams, as the district is known—is an agricultural village within hailing distance of the English Channel (locally, the faint tang of the sea mingles with the aroma of fertilizer), a nearly three-hour train ride from London, mostly through green fields dotted with livestock, that occasionally follows the coast. "Generations of the same families have been living here and working the land," says David Sheppard, whose home and architecture office—collectively called Cob Corner—sit on several acres of gently sloping land. Rural-agrarian though it may be, Ermington is still subject to the same rigorous planning and preservation rules that affect much of historic, picturesque England. "There is massive restriction against new construction," Sheppard affirms. Yet the rules—the governing aesthetic and the ways in which it can be interpreted—remain surprisingly flexible, in the right hands. "Everything doesn't have to be in the vernacular," the architect observes. "I think it's more to do with who's doing the designing."

So it was with Cob Corner. The principal structure, which Sheppard dates from about 1700 (flanked by a later-era lean-to and a twentieth-century tractor shed), was an open-front linhay barn, a typology found commonly in Devon and consisting of a first floor for sheltering livestock and a hayloft above. "And that was it," Sheppard says, "a very simple, traditional agricultural building, made from utilitarian materials taken mostly from the land—two columns, and a wall to hold up the pitched roof."

It was the latter two elements that, when he first visited the property, caught Sheppard's interest. The two cylindrical columns on one of the barn's long sides rose up from a one-story stone wall and tapered gracefully as they approached the roof. The opposite, dou-

OPPOSITE: Screens fashioned from boards serve as decorative elements, create privacy, and mitigate the impact of Cob Corner's extensive glazing.

ble-height wall—the so-called cob wall, from which the house takes its name—was the more intriguing, a prime example of seventeenth-century in situ construction. "The cob was made from clay on the site, a few stones, straw, and manure," Sheppard explains. "The straw acts as a fiber mesh, like fiberglass, so it's incredibly strong." The farmer's cows, the architect relates, would participate in the wall's creation. "They'd excrete onto their straw bedding, and that would all be taken out and mixed with the clay and stones. Then they'd have the animals walk back and forth across it to make the mix."

When asked why, after four centuries of exposure, the wall hadn't collapsed, Sheppard observes that, then as now, the core building material was skim-coated with lime render, a version of stucco. "But if you don't maintain it, the render will come off over time, and the cob will erode, which was starting to happen when I discovered it."

Sheppard's reinvention of the original suite of structures replaced the tractor shed with a new architecture studio; transformed the barn into his home's public areas, with a dining area and kitchen on the ground floor and the living room above it in the former hayloft (there is also a ground-floor master suite); and set two diminutive guest bedrooms in the old lean-to (which includes a new half-cylindrical structure enclosing a pair of tiny, wedge-shaped showers).

Before he could proceed, Sheppard had considerable structural work to do. The architect's major intervention involved building up the foundation of the barn so that it sat on a stone plinth, which concealed the new concrete floor slab and insulation. Knowing that he'd be using large expanses of glass, Sheppard took pains to ensure the plinth's stability, including a drainage system that prevented moisture build-up on the damp property (a stream runs past the studio)

SEVEN COB CORNER

95

ABOVE & BELOW:
Architect David
Sheppard purchased
a historic linhay barn, a
later-era addition, and
a modern tractor shed,
all dilapidated. His design
preserved the significant
architectural elements
and married them
to a modular building
system using repurposed
wood panels.

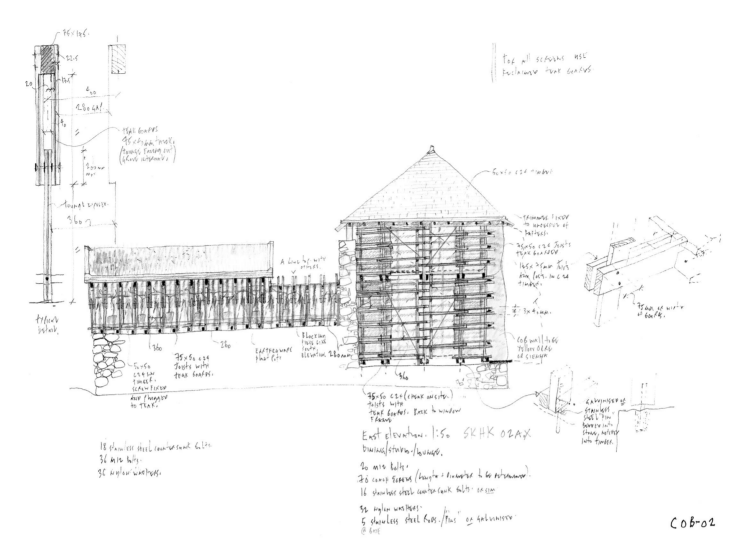

EAST ELEVATION. 1:50   SKHK 02AX
DINING/STUDIO./LOUNGE.

COB-02

while keeping the clay beneath the house "moist-ish so it doesn't shrink and produce cracking in the façade." The architect also restored the historic structures, a process that included resurfacing the cob wall with a yellow-ochre lime wash. "We used a traditional tool, sort of like a Tyrolean music box, that flicks the render onto the walls in a very artful way," he says.

Though Sheppard was careful to preserve the soul and spirit of what had been, both from natural inclination and in obeisance to the local preservation rules, Cob Corner's most interesting feature is in fact entirely contemporary. "Partly by luck, I went to this architectural antique dealer," Sheppard recalls. "And out back, he had this huge palette of identical hardwood panels that were used for storing engine mounts, maybe 250 in total. And I thought, *Fantastic, I'll design my whole building around them*, and bought the whole lot."

The aesthetic mileage Sheppard extracted from his discovery—which the architect treated as a de facto modular building system—was impressive. "We took the edges off, because they were mostly damaged," he says. "And then we were left with roughly 90-by-120-centimeter panels, which we put up in their natural state—minimum work, which enabled us to cover maximum area." Sheppard used the panels to clad the new studio (which replaced the modern-era tractor shed), separating them with narrow glazed channels that bring in daylight, and building a wall of panels that can be opened in various combinations to control the incoming light; he also used the panels to shape a snug entry vestibule/mudroom, with a stable door, to the main house.

Then Sheppard went an imaginative step further. Each of the panels was in fact constructed from ten identical boards held together by long bolts at the top and bottom. Having used large ex-

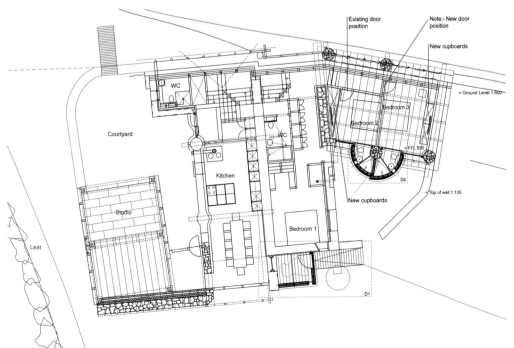

OPPOSITE & FOLLOWING PAGE: Sheppard replaced the tractor shed with his architecture studio. The rear wall features nine operable panels that modulate light and air.

ABOVE: Crisscrossing glass channels bring in light and sustain privacy.

101

Plan labels: Courtyard, WC, WC, Kitchen, Studio, Bedroom 1, Bedroom 2, Bedroom 3, Leat, Existing door position, Note:- New door position, New cupboards, New cupboards, + Ground Level 1.600, + FFL 550, + Top of wall 1.135, D1, D2

panses of glass on several of the house's façades, the architect decided he wanted to screen them in a way that would create privacy without obstructing light or views, while also producing an interesting layer of shadows on the glazing. So he took apart a number of the panels and refashioned the loose boards into screens that serve as an architectural decorative element, at once animating the exterior and fulfilling Sheppard's functional requirements. "When we put up the glass, it was too much," he recalls. "The shadow lines created by the slats give the glazing greater density, which diminishes its presence."

Elsewhere, the convergence of old and new is less obvious and more ambiguous, notably in the truss system that holds up the barn's pitched roof. The original A-shaped "collar" truss, with its pegged joinery and bits of tree bark supporting the ridge beam, remains in place. "I wanted to retain the fabric and recompose it with the new roof structure, but the trusses needed to be able to support the increased weight of the insulation and slates," the architect explains. "Originally I planned to put in a piece of steel or something like it, but then I thought I'd put a truss on a truss." Sheppard's simple "scissors" system—made from rough-hewn boards like the original— is attached to the collar with hand-hewn pegs and carries the extra weight. Though separated in time by centuries, "the two trusses read effectively as a single object."

Though they were designed to support a domestic program, Sheppard considered his new interventions—especially those that might qualify as craft objects, such as his custom-built wood pivot doors—from the perspective of vernacular architecture. "The whole idea was, I wanted expressions of an agricultural building using basic elements." The architect achieved this most strikingly in the winding stair that connects the kitchen and living levels. "I thought, well, how do you do a barn staircase?" the architect asks. "You just cut down a lot of trees and then build—and that's exactly how I approached it."

Sheppard is being somewhat disingenuous, as the steps and three landings, which wind upward around a cluster of muscular pillars, own a complexity that is at once confounding and appealing. The stair is also elegantly put together. "It's made from green oak, which is beautiful to work with because it chisels like cheese—you can make any joint very cleanly. The downside is, it shrinks and it moves—a *lot*." The splayed, cracked trio of vertical piers that anchor the composition bears him out. "You can never really know how it's going to happen, because wood moves as it wishes," he observes. Yet the entire unit, at once carefully designed and randomly torqued, suggests the raw power of a sculpture by Brâncuşi—an architecture-meets-nature collaboration that perfectly serves Sheppard's aspirations.

The architect's scheme interleaves the old and new in ways that depart significantly from typical barn-to-residence projects. "I've seen these conversions where outside it's a barn, and then you go in and all the original features, in particular the rawness, are absent," he says. "I wanted to retain the qualities and character of an agricultural building while still creating a modern dwelling." The latter he achieved via specifically architectural gambits: the Wrightian flavor of the screens against the glass and imposition of a modular building system on a more organically realized existing object. The former derives from a craft-based approach to design and making and, especially, "an economy of means, which I'm especially attracted to because, living where I do, a lot of my work has to convey that," Sheppard says. Materially rich, strongly crafted, aesthetically sophisticated, and entirely comfortable and functional, Cob Corner serves all of its gods with equal fidelity.

OPPOSITE: After several years in residence, Sheppard added an entry vestibule fashioned from leftover panels.

ABOVE: The silo-like half-cylinder holds two tiny showers—one for each guest room.

THIS PAGE: The numerous custom-crafted elements include louvers and doors. OPPOSITE: The exposed cob wall spans the kitchen and dining areas.

FOLLOWING SPREAD: Sheppard applied a new scissors truss to the original A-shaped design to support a heavier insulated roof.

THIS PAGE & OPPOSITE:
The raw sculpture of
the stair interweaves
careful planning and
skillful construction.
"My brother Terry took

my drawings and,
with all his skill as a
carpenter and builder,
made Cob what it is,"
Sheppard says.

111

8

Alabama: The Past Isn't Past

274 BRAGG AVENUE
auburn

+

MORGAN LOFT
birmingham

WHEN I FIRST BEGAN THIS BOOK, ONE OF MY HARD-and-fast rules was that I would not include any "adaptive reuse" projects, i.e., residences that had been previously put to other purposes. The reason grew out of what motivated my interest in hybrid homes in the first place: the coexistence of the past and present, and the ways in which interleaving the two can be mutually enlivening and enriching. In many, if not most, of the residential conversions that I have seen, there is not a serious engagement with history. Rather, one finds what might be described as an "historic moment"—a piece of equipment or unusual design detail that serves as a stand-alone cue regarding what the space had been; otherwise, the architects and/or residents have sought to take advantage of appealing spatial or material properties while banishing all evidence of previous habitation.

In three instances, however, I broke my own rule. The first, Cob Corner (page 94), was a mistake: What I believed to be a house for humans had originally been given to cows, a piece of information I somehow failed to process until I was standing in front of it. But this ended up working to my advantage, as David Sheppard, the architect/owner, was himself sensitive to the adaptive reuse problem and purposely avoided creating something that looked like a seventeenth-century agricultural building on the exterior and a chic contemporary residence within. Sheppard's effective scheme softened my resolve, and opened the way for 274 Bragg

OPPOSITE: 274 Bragg Avenue (ABOVE) and the Morgan loft (BELOW) share masonry exteriors, nonresidential histories, and significant positions in their different Alabama communities.

Avenue and the Morgan loft—the former originally a collection of commercial enterprises, the latter a onetime warehouse—located within a few hours of each other in Alabama.

"The past is never dead. It's not even past," William Faulkner famously wrote, and it can be too easy—especially for a Yankee like myself—to sentimentalize the South's brambled connection to its own history. As regards these residences, however, the author's observation seems apt. In each case, rather than "residentializing" the buildings, the owners embraced the existing conditions and the histories that underlay them, resulting in homes possessed of a powerful, even haunting sense of place.

With his wife, Elizabeth, and three young children, David Hill moved to Auburn from Charlottesville, where he'd been teaching part-time at the University of Virginia and working at landscape architect Julie Bargmann's innovative firm D.I.R.T. studio, in 2009. Essentially, Hill was replicating his situation, teaching landscape architecture at Auburn University while opening his own practice, called Hillworks: landscape + architecture.

While they enjoyed their new situation, the Hills didn't want to get too comfortable. "We were nervous about moving to suburbia, so we wanted to look for something that felt like who we are and not a little house with a front lawn," David recalls. On the day of his first job interview, "a real estate agent rode us

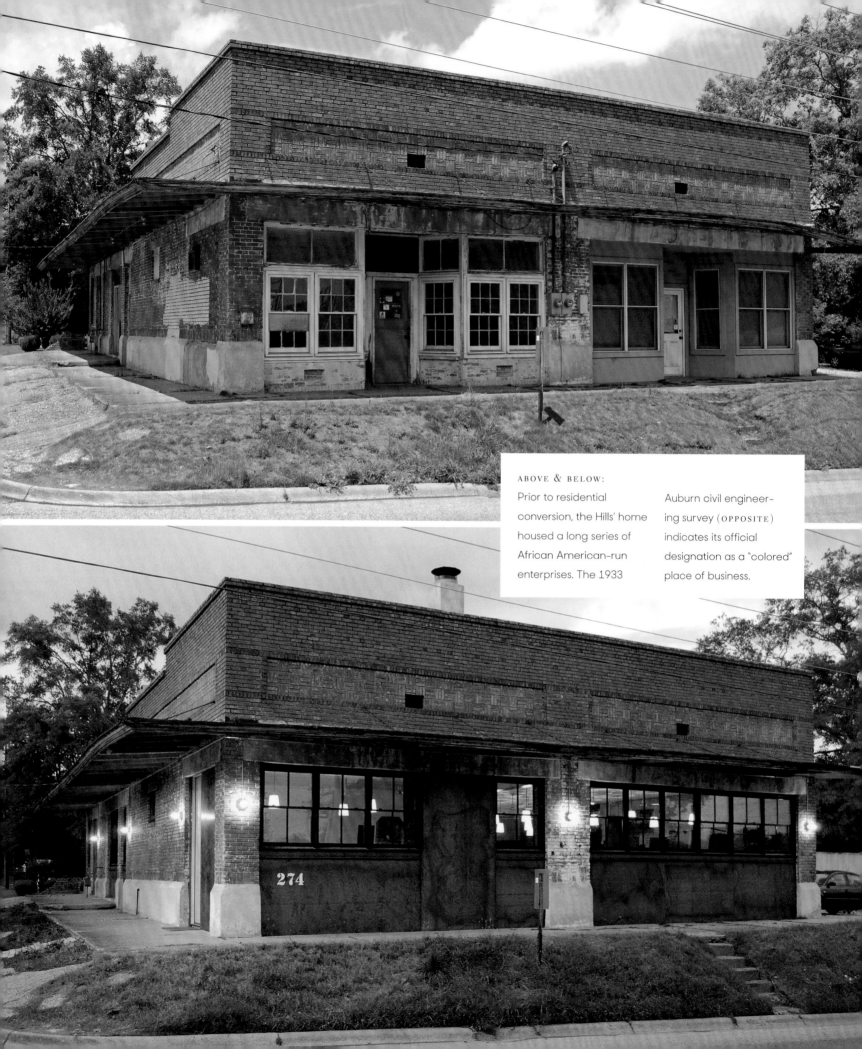

ABOVE & BELOW:
Prior to residential
conversion, the Hills' home
housed a long series of
African American-run
enterprises. The 1933

Auburn civil engineer-
ing survey (OPPOSITE)
indicates its official
designation as a "colored"
place of business.

274

around, and kept taking us to these places I wouldn't want to live in, and finally I said, 'We just went by this brick building, it looks like it needs some love, and that's kind of what we're interested in'"—and, to his great surprise, it proved to be available.

The structure in question, at the corner of Bragg Avenue and Frazier Street in one of Auburn's historic African American districts, was at the time a paint shop and storage facility, "and the epitome of a Southern corner store," Hill relates. He and Elizabeth "loved the big metal awning that wrapped around the front and side and shaded the concrete sidewalk—we were drawn to the idea of that as a social space and being able to spend time out there." Once they got inside the three-thousand-square-foot 1920 building, the Hills appreciated the nearly twelve-foot-high ceilings and foot-thick walls (which kept the place cool) and overall structural soundness, and the fact that the location was only a short walk to campus. "And we liked not only the racial and economic diversity of the area but also the aesthetic diversity," Hill says. "There isn't a neighborhood committee going around telling people to change the color of their doors."

Most of all, the couple was attracted to the idea of adaptive reuse. "Working at D.I.R.T., we were always talking about post-industrial this-and-that," and many of the firm's projects involved repurposing former factories and warehouses into public landscapes and social spaces. "I'd seen so many projects like that be incredibly fun and successful," Hill says. So despite their anxieties—the realtor had cautioned them that it was a "drug neighborhood" (which proved to be outdated information)—the Hills purchased the property in 2010.

Based on what they'd seen, the couple assumed the building had always been one or another sort of industrial facility—"The only historic thing that was legible was the brick," the architect says. The Hills planned to research the building's history, "to make our project

more rich." But they didn't expect to discover very much. "Really, we thought we were just going to do a cool loft."

The research, however, changed everything. "There were two documents we discovered that flipped our minds over," Hill recalls. "In 1933, the Auburn civil engineering department did a survey of the city, and the map they produced had a key on it. And we saw that 274 Bragg Avenue had a mark indicating that it was a business, and another line indicating that it was a 'colored' business." The other document the Hills consulted was the 1928 Sanborn Map. Introduced in the 1860s and used to assess fire insurance liability, the maps gave exceptionally detailed information regarding individual properties and their environs; studying the Sanborn, the Hills discovered that 274 Bragg had been divided into four separate businesses, the largest of which had been a pool hall. "And we thought, Wow!" Hill recalls. "That's history we can get excited about."

Working from phone books and city directories, the Hills identified multiple proprietors involved with the four leasable spaces. They discovered that the pool room, which faced Bragg, had eventually become King's Kongo Klub, with red-painted walls embedded with glitter; that the corner concern beside it had functioned as multiple restaurants; the narrow space on Frazier served as a barbershop where a Mister Cecil commanded the principal chair; and that the enterprise at the far end had housed a cab company, a restaurant, and a fish store. Over half a century, says Hill, "there was an incredibly high turnover, and that tells you as much about this place as the business names do. It's a similar story to what you find in many Southern towns."

Fired up, the Hills hung a sign requesting that anyone with knowledge about the building get in touch; and as they proceeded with demolition, the storytellers began to arrive, bearing riches. "There was one guy who stood out in front of where the restaurant

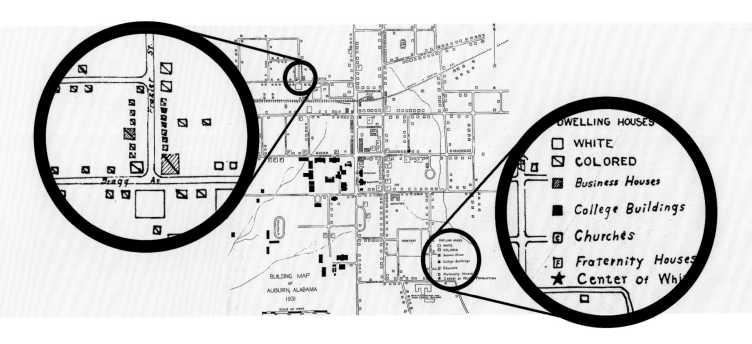

h695 S Gay (A)
--Richd S jr studt r695 S Gay (A)
Harlem Cabs (E P Owen) branch of radio
   cab 907 S Railroad av (O)
**HARLEM POOL ROOM (Charlie H
   Brock), Pool Tables, Cold Drinks,
   Music Box, Bragg cor Frazier av (A)**
Harley Herbert E studt h200 Elm apt 6
   (A)
Harman Ronald studt r125 Toomer
Harmon Chas Mrs sten Auburn Univ
--Wm E (Jonnye Z) h130 S Ross (A)

(T-116)

IN
AUBURN
(COLORED)
QUICK, COURTEOUS EFFICIENT SERVICE

TAXI
Service
6 COURTEOUS DRIVERS TO SERVE YOU
887-3125
FRAZIER ST. CAB CO.
TOM OSCAR LYNCH - MGR.
FRAZIER   AUBURN

ABOVE: The owners searched old phone books and city directories for information about the structure's former tenants. A corner restaurant (LEFT) became part of the living room.

FOLLOWING SPREAD: The main living/kitchen/dining zone occupies what had been a pool hall. The huge sliding steel door closes off the rest of the living room and restores the original spatial relationship.

was and said, 'I learned how to be a man *right here*,'" Hill relates with a mischievous smile. "I thought, Hmm, this could go many ways, but it turned out that his father worked at the sawmill across the street, and he and his buddies used to have breakfast every day at the restaurant and then play dominoes on this bench that was out front. And this guy would go with his dad, and learn the good, the bad, and the ugly from the older folks. And then there was Mr. Spencer, who's in his eighties—his grandfather started Spencer Lumber, which was part of Auburn Ice and Coal," Hill continues, warming to his tale. "He said that one Saturday evening, a fight broke out between two guys in the pool hall and spilled out into the street—he saw one guy slit the other guy's throat with a knife. And he said, 'Don't you know, not one week later, those two guys were back playing pool together—it was just that kind of place.'" Eventually the couple's ad hoc oral history project and research yielded so much information that they created what Hill describes as "a science-fair kind of timeline," which documents the occupants of each space from 1920 until the family took ownership—complete with hot links leading to print ads, phone book listings, and other vintage materials—and posted it on the Hillworks website.

Most significantly, the Hills' research transformed their vision of the renovation. "When we thought it was just a warehouse, we said, *Well, we can work with this wall, but those walls are a pain in the butt, so let's get rid of 'em*," Hill explains. Instead, though they conceived of the building as a comprehensive residence, the Hills chose to retain many of the old partitions, so that the "ghosts" of the four original businesses, their proportions and relationships, still existed. The couple did this, moreover, at the expense of their own convenience, especially as regards the barbershop, which remains intact. "It makes this kind of strange space," Hill admits, "because it's too small to be a major room and too large to be a corridor—it took a while to figure out what to do with it." (Ultimately the family conceived of it as a "study hall" sited between the children's bedrooms and shared bath.) The Hills' other major design strategy was "to make legible all of our moves," says David, notably by using raw steel to fill in openings or make doors. "That way, people won't be confused and think, well, that's historic brick."

The Hills deftly stitched their domestic program into the original plan. In front, they combined the corner restaurant and pool room into an L-shaped living/dining area (a wall-size sliding steel door can restore the original separation). The rear of the pool room incorporates what Hill calls the "kitchen cube," a volume with the open kitchen on one side and the master bath and closets on the other, facing David and Elizabeth's bedroom suite in the rear, where the cab company serviced its cars. On one side of the barbershop-turned-study hall (ac-

cessed via a portal near the kitchen), two children's bedrooms fill the space once occupied by the cab company's office. On the other side, a third bedroom and shared children's bath fill the rear of the old restaurant space. Though the Hills resisted giving the concrete floor a loft-style polish, opting instead for a dark-stained bamboo, they preserved the original pressed-tin ceiling in the public rooms, adding hanging lights to make the place feel more like a pool hall. Many of the walls retain their layered, patinated finishes (the silhouette of an old toilet appears in the master bedroom); when paint was used, the Hills largely selected preexisting colors. Wherever possible, iconic elements were preserved. "Even though the awning was in bad shape, we kept it," Hill says, indicating its warped undulations. "There's a character to the way it wiggles up and down."

The outcome is not without bumps. "The whole place is larger than we needed," Hill admits, especially the children's zone, a consequence of keeping the barbershop. "We felt it was important, and we're better for having it, but if we'd taken down the walls we could have had smaller bedrooms and an office with its own entry." The other issue has to

do with the building's presence on two well-traveled streets: To maintain privacy, many of the windows have been made smaller or raised above head height, leaving the place feeling somewhat hermetic and daylight-deficient. "There were two doors on the front, and with Bragg now being a state highway, we decided to use the older door around the side," Hill says. Large cabinets now cover the living room wall, with high windows partially blocked by pictures. "We wanted what we did to be a public story. But we also wanted our privacy."

Which suggests the paradox of a project like 274 Bragg. Though the neighbors have expressed appreciation for what they've done, and the Hillworks website has made the building's history available in detail, what was for nearly a century a significant component of the area's social fabric now rests in private hands; as often happens with commercial-to-residential conversions, the lively corner has in a sense gone mute. But not forever, Hill believes. "I think we've added to the building's history and allowed the story to continue. But we're only stewards for a little while—eventually we'll get out of the way, and let the next person decide what comes next."

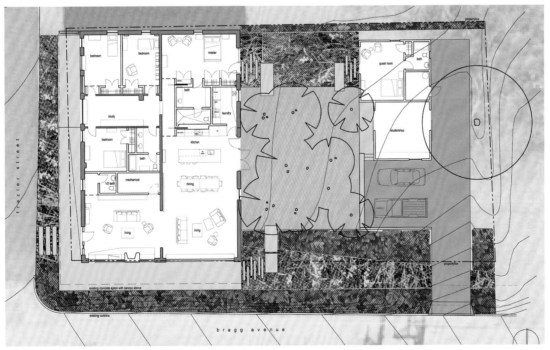

OPPOSITE: Though
it would have better
served their needs to
reconfigure the space,
the Hills kept the former
barbershop intact.
ABOVE: In the master
suite, a cab company
once serviced its fleet.

BEFORE I DEPART FOR BIRMINGHAM TO MEET CHERYL Morgan, a former architecture professor at Auburn University, David Hill talks about her. "She's just a very special, unique person," he says. "Without her, Birmingham would not be what it is today."

Over coffee the next morning in her loft, in a light-industrial zone of the city, Morgan contextualizes Hill's hosanna. In 1997, she became the director of the university's Birmingham-based Urban Studio, a program that brought students largely unfamiliar with cities to the big town, as it were, to study the urban fabric and "do hypothetical projects in context," Morgan recalls. "We identified things we thought should be part of the dialogue if Birmingham was going to move forward." One of these was a no-man's-land, a vacant former train yard that was ultimately transformed into the award-winning Railroad Park, Birmingham's great public showplace. "It was something everybody laughed at," Morgan says. "But we kept coming up with designs and wouldn't let people forget about it." The studio's ground-seeding eventually produced a champion in city government, who set the project in motion—"and today there's $400 million in development going on around that park." Describing herself as a "stubborn optimist," Morgan says, "the project gave us confidence that we could do something exceptional and didn't have to settle."

Whatever it did for Birmingham, Morgan's experience influenced her loft, it would seem, two essential ways. "One of the hallmarks of design development is getting out of the way of whatever needs to happen," she observes, "so a building can do what it's supposed to do well." The second lesson is even more apt. "Place-making is the point, not object-making. You want to do a glorious building. But if that's the point, you've missed the larger opportunity."

In the middle 2000s, Morgan decided it was time to make a new place of her own. "I had lived on First Avenue North, in the first building that had converted to lofts in Birmingham," she recalls. Morgan is an adventurous, restless spirit, and when things started to get too comfortable, "I said, *I'm ready to move to the next edge.*" In 2004, with the help of a realtor/developer friend, she began nosing around First Avenue South, a light-industrial boulevard comprised of warehouses, garages, and metal fabricators. "This was the next obvious place," Morgan says. "Design professionals were moving in, just down the street is the practice facility for our ballet, and about

ABOVE: Morgan's loft occupies roughly two-thirds of a former warehouse. OPPOSITE: As the ceiling was collapsing at the building's rear, Morgan removed it entirely to create an enclosed garden, with a pivot door opening onto the back alley.

four blocks away is an area called Pepper Place, which has a huge Saturday farmers' market."

Morgan's building wasn't in fact available—her realtor knew that the then-owners, who fabricated aluminum windows and doors, were planning to relocate sometime in the near future—but after touring the place, she said she'd be willing to wait. Built in 1910 as a warehouse, the 140-by-50-foot, two-story masonry structure filled the lot and, excepting the modest second-floor offices overlooking the street, was essentially open, double-height space from front to back. A grid of wooden support columns held the roof up and lightly divided the vast interior, barn-style, into three bays. "The middle one was twelve feet wide, and the ones on the side were seventeen feet," Morgan recalls; the center bay was in fact the transportation artery through the structure, with a hoist rail above and dense, heavy, red oak floors (as opposed to the heart pine on the sides), supported by extra joists, below. "It was clear the builders had designed it to accommodate the weights they were anticipating," Morgan explains. "You could back a railroad car in here."

BELOW & OPPOSITE: A new wall of glass contrasts with the unchanged original construction, and brings abundant light into the otherwise nearly windowless space.

The building had been designed with consideration, and not a little elegance, in other ways. "The column grid—the bay widths—were well disposed for flexibility in the use of space," Morgan says. "The roof was sloped for drainage, and when you examined the capitals atop the columns—they're hundred-year-old heart pine—you saw that the trapezoidal shape wasn't perfect; they'd adjusted it slightly to accommodate the slope. There was the evidence of craft—the makers had thought to give it dignity."

When Morgan toured the structure, "it was packed with stuff," including a mezzanine that partially covered one of the side bays, "and I had to shuffle sideways—you couldn't actually get to the back corner, where the low part of the roof was caving in." But the urban pioneer was sold. Rather than fixing the damaged part of the roof, "my notion was that I'd just peel it off and open that up to create outdoor space."

Morgan's time in, her commitment to the city, paid off personally. "My realtor, a friend from the Urban Studio, had been active in Birmingham for forty years, so he knew about the building," she says.

"I'd built relationships with people who helped me figure out the financing, some of the hoops with the zoning. And," she admits, "I was lucky. I could never have afforded this if it wasn't in Birmingham, with our disgustingly low property taxes, plus my timing."

Morgan closed on the building in 2006, and by necessity developed it incrementally. "This was an industrial area, and if I couldn't get a zoning change I was going to flip the place," she says. After receiving a "spot re-zoning," an eight-month effort, Morgan spent half a year renovating the original second-floor front office, which she rented to husband-and-wife landscape architects. "That gave me an income stream, so I could start saving money to do my house." Working with an architecture firm called Design Initiative (now her second tenant, occupying first-floor space below the landscapers), Morgan finished the project in 2011.

Spatially, her loft is lavish—astonishingly so, incorporating a 49-by-49-foot main floor (the ceiling rises from twelve to fifteen feet), a 900-square-foot mezzanine, and a 50-by-30-foot exterior courtyard, plus abundant library, work, and storage space. Yet what is most striking is what Morgan hasn't done: For all its creature comforts, the home feels nearly as raw as a squat—suffused with the power, and purity, of material, space, and history.

Morgan neither refinished the floors nor painted the walls. "Nobody goes barefoot when they visit my house," she quips, looking out over the exposed 1,500 square feet of scarred, splintered boards. "Also the roof sheds," Morgan adds. "I put a new one on, but the joists between the planks retained gravel from the original, so every once in a while a rock will fall out of the sky." The textured walls ("they shed a bit too") are made of hollow clay tile attached to the outer brick skin, and everywhere evidence of the building's history is revealed. The eye is quickly drawn to a gray, nose-like protuberance sticking out from a wall like an outsider-art version of a Robert Gober sculpture. "That's where the water-cooled saw for cutting the aluminum was," Morgan explains. "The residual wet, hot metal stuck to the wall." The porous, unfinished surfaces dampen sound in the room. And rather than restricting the flow, says Morgan, "the columns give me a way to define zones. I've got use, vacancy, use, vacancy," pointing out furniture arrangements in alternation with voids, "and that's very intentional—I use space that's not occupied as a way to understand

space that is." Like the overall intervention, Morgan's furniture plan is carefully conceived, but because of the rawness of the loft, it feels artless and opportunistic—as though she'd found an abandoned warehouse and, liking the vibe (and the ghosts), simply moved in.

The room's only fixed program is the open kitchen, near the new wall of south-facing glass separating the loft from the courtyard. With one exception, the rest of Morgan's home—the pantry, utility closet, guest bath, and office/guest room—is tucked under the mezzanine, in what the architects dubbed "the box." Wrapped in a nondescript Luan plywood, the zone incorporates all the areas requiring closed doors. "I love volume, but I live very low in space," says Morgan, "so the office is comfortable when I'm focused on my work." Having discrete rooms also facilitates more flexible climate control: Morgan maintains two HVAC systems—one for the box, the other for everything else—which enables her to fine-tune temperature.

ABOVE: The original hoist rail remains above the center bay and passes through the glass wall before snaking its way to the garden's pivot door (PREVIOUS PAGES).

That single exception is Morgan's private suite, which sits atop the mezzanine and is lightly divided into sleeping, bath, and dressing areas. "It's the balance between the 'nest' rooms underneath and the big open volume," she says of the linear band of uncovered zones, enclosed on the loft-facing side by a Luan-clad partition, entirely open on the other (the bed is in fact completely exposed). As laid out, the mezzanine is spacious enough to have circulation on both sides and keep the bath and dressing room open and easily accessed but also private and invisible.

Perhaps the loft's most considered element is the bi-level courtyard, which sits between the new floor-to-ceiling glass and the masonry wall separating the building lot from the service alley in back. Much thought was given to where, precisely, the indoor/outdoor line should fall, with the glass standing inches from a row of columns rather than between them, "so the new stuff is not engaging, but residing with," Morgan says. The alley wall received a stabilizing concrete cap and a new aperture was inserted with a pivoting panel, made from salvaged red oak flooring, that is meant

ABOVE: Morgan left the floor, walls, and beams as she found them. The dark spot on the wall, with its nose-like protuberance, was the site of a saw used for cutting aluminum.

to be the home's proper entrance; a down-sloping walkway connects the door to the deck, forming a bridge over a lower-level "Zen garden," with a pebbled bed, water channels, and aluminum planter boxes. With the hoist rail snaking above and a row of old columns supporting the beams that carry the rain gutters, the court stands as the residence's most elegant interleaving of past and present, a contemplative zone within a larger oasis.

The Hills' residence became a vehicle for discovering their community, whereas Morgan's loft grew out of her long personal and professional experience in Birmingham. But both homes reflect what Morgan impressed upon her Urban Studio students: the importance of getting out of the way of what a building wants to be, and of focusing not on the object but rather the place. "I clearly made decisions about how to occupy the space," Morgan says. "But I didn't want it to feel self-conscious. And"—like the Hills—"I respect that the building was here before me, and after me, who knows?"

Pointing out her kitchen sink, Morgan relates that it was salvaged from a Georgia farmhouse where she lived as a teenager. "When my parents remodeled the house, they leaned it up against a tree, and it stood there for forty years, until I went and got it," she says. "That's become one of my judgments of good design: Can an object, or a building, have a second life? If something can only be what it was originally meant to be, maybe it was overdesigned." Connected to this interesting existential question, Morgan believes, "is the idea that you can continue to discover things about a place over time." That capacity for change—to change use and perception, to come out of the past and embrace the future—threads through the narrative of both these Alabama homes.

FOLLOWING SPREAD: Morgan used an existing mezzanine to create an upstairs master suite, and a pantry, guest bath, and office underneath.

EIGHT ALABAMA: THE PAST ISN'T PAST

Morgan left her bed
exposed, and concealed
the bath, which is open
on the side facing the

wall. This preserves
privacy, and guards
against groggy late-
night accidents.

9

COTSWOLDS HOUSE
cranham, england

"I DO TEND TO CALL IT THE MARMITE HOUSE," says Richard Found's housekeeper as she opens the door to the architect's country cottage, "because people either love it or hate it." The residence, at the lower end of a sixteen-acre, steeply sloping valley in the Cotswolds, is in fact well suited to opposing extremes of response, as the house itself is a collision of opposites: an early-nineteenth-century gamekeeper's cottage with head-scraping ceilings and diminutive rooms linked to a tripartite, angular modernist volume, distinguished by a seventy-five-foot-long wall of floor-to-ceiling frameless glass. Yet the totality works surprisingly well, thanks not only to Found's imagination and resourcefulness but also to the beneficial influence that restrictions—even unexpected and severe ones—can have on a creative endeavor.

"I've always loved the country, and I like being around water," the London-based architect says, explaining the instant appeal the property held for him as a country retreat. "There are two lakes, and a stream that gives you running water for trout—I do a lot of fishing—and in the summer there's a waterfall that you hear." The cottage itself, set on a terraced slope arranged with small outbuildings and backed up against the beech forest that abuts the open land, "was in a real state," Found recalls. "The wood floor was disintegrating, and it was quite dilapidated overall." To Found and family, this didn't matter: It was the great sloping sweep of land that they loved, and the architect and his wife planned to demolish the cottage and rebuild to take better advantage of the site.

It was not the cottage that was demolished, however, but Found's plans for it. "As soon as I mentioned the thought of taking it down, the local planning council spot-listed it"—meaning that, as a Grade II protected structure, it had to be preserved. (When the

OPPOSITE: Prevented from demolishing the original cottage, Richard Found made a virtue of necessity, styling his addition to resemble a modernist version of traditional retaining walls.

architect got the news, he was driving; realizing that he'd purchased a major piece of premium property that suddenly had what amounted to a deal-breaking restriction, Found's back seized, and he had to be pried out of the car.) Neither could Found construct a new house at a remove from the cottage: the planning and conservation mandarins insisted than any new building be conceived as an "addition" to the original, which, the architect recalls, "had to remain the dominant feature on the site."

Found's solution, arrived at "after a year and a half of negotiations," proved to be an adroit contemporary spin on the local vernacular. Taking his cue from the existing conditions, the architect conceived of the extension as a series of abstracted retaining walls made from the same signature Cotswold stone as the cottage, which descend the slope behind the building and actually leave the back of the new construction buried in the landscape. The size of the addition, moreover, was more or less equal to the total square footage of the existing shed buildings on the site, which Found was allowed to demolish. Presented with a structure that played second fiddle to the historic original, clad in a familiar local material and styled as a traditional agricultural wall—no bigger than what had previous existed and half-submerged besides—the planners acquiesced.

The new wing is spare and simple in both its planning and execution: It moves down the property in a linear fashion, with the eastern four-bedroom wing at the high point; the central entry volume in the middle, on the same level as the cottage (and connecting the two); and the living-and-kitchen great room a few steps down to the west. As the rear of the structure is submerged in the hillside, most of the glazing is on the southern façade overlooking the valley; a pair of long

THIS PAGE & OPPOSITE:
In addition to extensive
sitework, Found's
scheme involved the
restoration of the
cottage, which he
completed prior to
beginning the extension.

skylights brings natural light down into the circulation spaces at the back. The palette is equally restrained, almost entirely poured-in-place concrete and white Corian, with a few plaster walls in the domestic areas. Rather than conventional windows, the bedrooms feature floor-to-ceiling glass doors that can pocket away completely, opening each space entirely to nature (each can be covered by a shutter "with per-forations just small enough to keep out insects, but large enough to get ventilation," says Found, "so in summer you can sleep with the window open and not wake up with a badger alongside you"). In the great room, the stunning, L-shaped glass walls, entirely unobstruct-ed by columns or mullions, offer a CinemaScopic view of the lower landscape and convert the interior into what Found calls "a reverse terrarium, because you get deer and wildlife coming right up to the glass and looking in at you."

Found also applied his minimalist sensibility to the cottage, but used his rigorously modern language to tell a historic story. Here the

simple palette is comprised of new plaster and old wood, the rooms are intimate and the windows small, and the character and texture derive from the original building elements and the simple craft of the details. Though the building methods are in tune with the origi-nal—"the stone tile roof is insulated with sheep's wool, which would have been true when it was first completed," the architect notes—the execution remains as impeccable as in the addition; and while the effect is "cottage cozy," the judiciously curated, just-so décor makes the place seem utterly contemporary.

Above all, there is the unexpected benefit that never would have materialized had the architect gotten his way: The presence of the cottage at the approximate midpoint of the project at once makes the extension seem smaller than it is and shapes the views. "If you're down by the pond and look back up at the place, you only see the old building and the new living room part," Found observes. "And when you arrive from the road above, you just get

the cottage and the bedrooms—you're unaware of the other half. So the whole addition's about five thousand square feet, but unless you're directly in front of the house, you're really only seeing half of it at any given time."

The project, which involved landfill in front of the cottage and extensive site excavation for the extension, proved complicated to execute, the new part in particular—an effort of fourteen months, more than twice the time required to renovate the cottage. "When you're dealing with poured-in-place concrete, absolutely everything has to be considered, down to the power sockets," says Found. The house was also an engineering challenge, in particular the cantilevered roof that makes possible the living room's long window wall. "The glazers said that we could only allow for a five millimeter toler- ance," the architect recalls. "So you can imagine the fun and games of designing the structure, knowing

you only had a tiny bit of flexibility—and that you could have two hundred people partying on the roof."

In the end, of course, the effort paid off. "When we finally moved in, I think I was most surprised by the view," says Found. "And the tranquility. We use the whole place," he adds. "We do quite a bit of entertaining, and when people are down for the weekend, we go into the cottage to play games—it's a nice contrast of spaces."

Quite apart from the pleasures of habitation, the architect's old- new hybrid has been widely praised, not least by the Royal Institute of British Architects, which gave the cottage a National Award in 2012. "In hindsight, it would have been a big mistake, tearing down the cottage," Found admits— and his reluctance-to-creative-riches story reminds one of Shakespeare's wise observation in *Twelfth Night*, that "some are born great, some achieve greatness, and oth- ers have greatness thrust upon them."

OPPOSITE & ABOVE: An unexpected benefit of retaining the cottage was that its midpoint position in the plan makes the entirety less imposing— side views reveal only half the house.

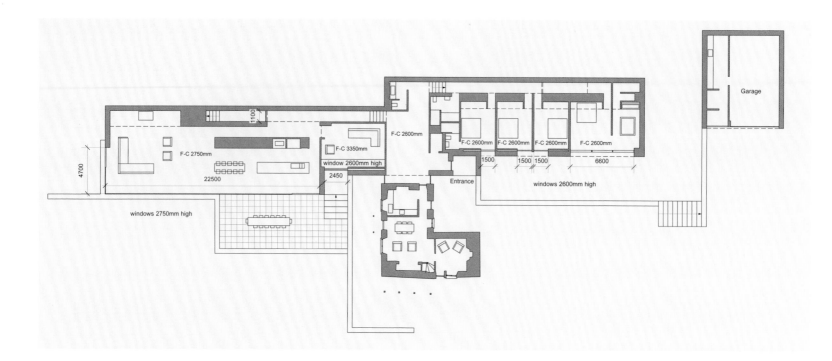

F-C 2750mm

F-C 3350mm

F-C 2600mm

F-C 2600mm   F-C 2600mm   F-C 2600mm   F-C 2600mm

Garage

Entrance

window 2600mm high

windows 2600mm high

windows 2750mm high

4700

1100

22500

2450

1500   1500   1500   6600

OPPOSITE: A narrow glass link separates the stacked-stone rear of the cottage from the addition's poured-concrete entry.

RIGHT: Long skylights bring daylight into the back of the new building, which is buried in the hillside.

RIGHT: The new living/ kitchen/dining space offers panoramic views of the property through walls of frameless glass. "I know it's a cliché," Found says, "but the relationship between the cottage and the new building is what's exciting."

LEFT: The monastic bedrooms in the addition open completely to the landscape.

OPPOSITE & BELOW: Though Found's renovation preserved many of the cottage's original elements, his spare modern aesthetic predominates.

10

LONGBRANCH
key peninsula, washington

REFLECTING ON THE PROPERTY THAT HAS BEEN in his family for a century, and the nearly six-decade-old house at the center of it—a project he began in his teens and is still revising in his seventies—the architect Jim Olson says, "You don't worry out here about what you're wearing, or whether or not the living room has been picked up. My family has always said, 'It doesn't matter—it's Longbranch.'"

Longbranch the town, from which Olson's house takes its name, lies some ninety minutes outside Seattle, near the end of the sixteen-mile-long Key Peninsula, an arm of land reaching into Puget Sound. Olson's property, which his mother's parents purchased in 1912, descends steeply from the road, through stands of tall, aromatic fir and cedar trees that surround the house, to a flat expanse of lawn. A few yards beyond it lies Puget Sound and, across the water, set off by low-lying land masses, a view of Mt. Rainier that can only be described as conversation-stopping. "My grandparents built their summer cottage right here," Olson says, indicating the remains of a foundation near the stony beach, "because when you sat on the porch, you looked across the water at the mountain, and that was very important to them. When I was a kid, that was talked about all the time—you really noticed how things looked from certain vantage points."

The architect's many sepia-toned family photos reveal the storybook pleasures of country living at the start of the twentieth century, which mixed roughing it with a certain Victorian formality. "You came by ferry to the Longbranch dock, which is about a mile from here, and then got into these big wooden rowboats, and quite often they were dressed up." In one image, sixteen family members sit the full length of a downed tree projecting out above the sound, the gents wearing creased trousers and ankle-high shoes, the ladies in

OPPOSITE: Begun as a one-room bunkhouse in 1959 with the structure at right, Jim Olson's lake house was ultimately extended three times, most recently in 2012.

long skirts and black stockings; the very last fellow, feet held just above the water and grinning at the camera, sports a bowtie. And there was no swimming, though this had nothing to do with propriety. "The water is ice cold," Olson says. "You'd freeze to death."

The original house burned down in 1962, but by then Olson's parents and aunt and uncle had taken over the adjacent land and built their own homes, innocent of global warming, virtually at the water's edge. His folks' place, an A-frame designed by a Tacoma architect named Mary Davis, isn't to Olson's liking, but he enthuses about the other dwelling, the work of the northwestern modernist Paul Kirk. "My parents' chalet was aggressive, whereas Kirk believed in sitting lightly on the land," he says, gesturing at the modest cottage, a cousin to LA's postwar Case Study projects. "I've always loved the simple lines playing off the organic forms of the landscape. This was the sort of thing that interested me."

An interest that, by 1959, was aspirational: Olson, then eighteen, was in his first year of architecture school, and the Seattle-based Kirk "was one of my heroes." Olson's enthusiasm is evident in his very first project, the fourteen-by-fourteen-foot box that became Longbranch's cornerstone. "My parents wouldn't let me design their house; they didn't think I was old enough," the architect recalls. But to execute the Davis plan, "they had to bulldoze part of the property and tear down an existing bunkhouse. And my Dad gave me $500 and said, 'Go build a new bunkhouse'—that was my consolation prize."

The outcome was the ultimate in simplicity: board-and-batten cedar siding, windows taken from another structure, decking on two sides, no electricity or plumbing. "Just six bunk beds," Olson recalls. "It was a place to sleep, nothing more." Yet Kirk's influence, and the student's ambitions, remain evident in the posts and beams that

lightly enclose the decks, to form a tectonic approximation of the woods and make the shed seem bigger. "It's quite a beautiful building," Olson says, laughing. "I always loved it."

Remarkably, the bunkhouse remained more or less as it was for twenty-two years, though "somewhere in the 1970s," following his marriage to his second (and current) wife, Katherine, the architect added power and installed "a little kitchen unit, with a sink, fridge, and stove, over in a corner," which Olson set behind a wall that also concealed a closet. "We started using it like a miniature summer house," he recalls. "We had two double beds so if we had friends out they'd have a place to sleep." Though Olson's parents were next door, he seems not to have depended on their comforts. "We had a toilet set on chrome legs—you'd take it out and dig a hole somewhere. Life," he sighs, "has gotten so fancy."

By 1982, Olson had some money, and with the charms of single-room occupancy fraying, his family was ready for fancy—though not much: to the bunkhouse the architect added two, comparably diminutive, free-standing pavilions. One, a short flight of stairs up the

ABOVE: Longbranch today. OPPOSITE: Olson's house, built on land that has been in his family for over a century, is steps away from Puget Sound.

hill, contained a bathtub, sink, and toilet; the other, a few steps across the original deck, held a bed. "To us, this represented Shangri-La," Olson recalls. As in 1959, and despite the Spartan simplicity of the addition, architecture came into play; the post-and-beam language was continued, and Olson made both new structures open to the landscape via generously sized, uncurtained windows and skylights. Significantly, the distinction between old and new remained exposed. "I didn't connect the three objects—you had to go out to go in—and I liked the idea of the old parts looking old, because they *were* old."

And so things remained for a generation, other than a minor redo of the kitchen and replacement of part of the bunkhouse glazing with glass doors. But as the new century dawned, the Olsons were feeling their age. "When we built it, walking outside in the middle of the night and going up slippery stairs to use the bathroom didn't seem like a problem," Olson explains. "In your sixties, it's a problem. And we'd always thought about having a beautiful living room." So in 2003, the couple "put a big hat over the old house," in the architect's formulation, in the form of a tall linear volume wide enough

to enclose half the bunkhouse and the open space between it and the sleeping pavilion, but much longer: stretching from a new living room that projected out over the hillside toward Puget Sound (with wall-size glass on three sides) and flowing in the opposite direction, past the bunkhouse and down a hall lined with utility spaces to a bathroom in the rear. The layered, planar design referenced the existing architecture, with board-and-batten plywood on the inner and outer walls, and exposed posts and crisscrossing beams, but the overall effect was grand: The soaring ceiling height—space for space's sake—conveyed luxury, notably in the bath with its full-height window, offering a vertical natural vista, at the foot of the tub.

The addition delivered the requisite comfort and convenience. But it also built on the idea of temporal simultaneity, notably with the partial swallowing up of the bunkhouse, which became a kind of historic fragment within the new, much taller space. Many people collect objects that reflect their histories, placing them in rooms as reminders of happy times. Olson had done the same thing with architecture.

"So there we were, and we loved it," Olson says—until the march of time, and the need to think ahead, stirred the architect's pencil

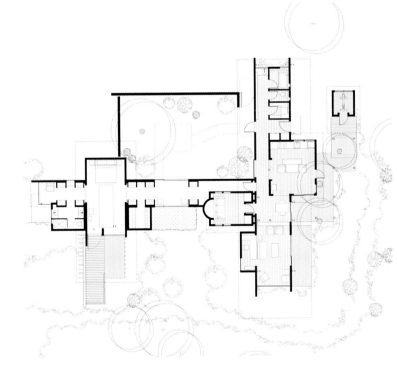

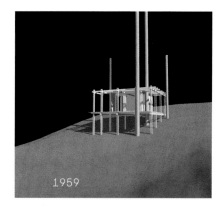

1959

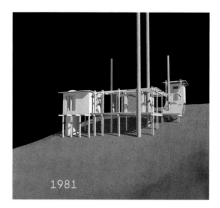

1981

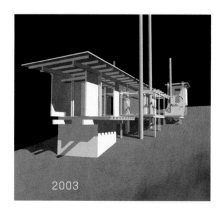

2003

ABOVE & RIGHT: Olson
began with a one-room
structure in 1959, then
expanded Longbranch
in 1981 and 2003.

RIGHT: The house
Olson's grandparents
built after purchasing
the property in 1912.

FOLLOWING SPREAD:
The 1981 iteration
featured two new
freestanding pavilions,
one for the bathroom,
the other enclosing the
sleeping quarters.

anew. Though the sleeping pavilion provided a measure of privacy, the Olsons' houseguests typically crashed in different parts of the living room and kitchen, with everyone sharing the bath. "And we thought, wouldn't it be nice if we had our own wing, so that people could be here and Katherine and I could get away," Olson explains. Though the couple has kept a condominium in Seattle's Pioneer Square for three decades, "Longbranch was becoming more our home than the place in town, and I wanted to have a real office, so people could come out and work." Finally, and most significantly, "We want to come here as long as we're alive, and we're assuming we'll live to be one hundred," Olson says. Creating accommodations for an on-site caregiver would facilitate the centenarian dream.

And so in 2012 Olson pushed off in a new direction—literally—roughly doubling the size of Longbranch with a new, two-story wing, set perpendicular to the old house, that extends past the sleeping pavilion and terminates in a grand master suite that echoes the 2003 living room addition, cantilevering out over the landscape (though with even more drama).

Given the old house's informality, the new wing's most unexpected quality is its sense of procession, notably in the circulation space connecting the existing structure to the master bedroom, which serves as Katherine's library. This Olson took from his residential work. "A lot of my houses are almost museum-like," he observes. "You have these galleries lined with columns, and you get a ceremonial feeling as you move through them. And I thought, let's do that at a more intimate scale, and use the library to create a sense of cadence." Though there are relatively few bookcases, the library remains a soothing place to relax, with windows facing the sound on one side and glass sliders opening onto a new enclosed courtyard on the other. The architect also stained both the interior and exterior cladding a dark color, "so

that it disappears—you're kind of going through the woods between one house and the next."

If the library is a metaphoric forest walk, then the master bedroom serves as the clearing in which the branch canopy disappears. "This is the highest ceiling in the house," Olson affirms. "We'd never had a nice big bedroom before, and we just decided for once to do it." The room is lined with five different sizes of rough-cut spruce boards, found by Olson in a recycling yard, and installed by the carpenters in a random order—an abstraction of a forest clearing—and the circulation spine begun by the library continues through it to the bath area, dividing the space into a cozy zone for the bed and a more exposed sitting area that opens onto a terrace.

On the level below, Olson set a combination office and self-contained guest suite, with its own kitchen and washer/dryer—"Katherine said, 'I don't want to run an inn'"—and though the rooms are partially buried in the hillside, the eleven-foot ceilings and south-facing windows "make guests feel special, and not like they're sleeping in the basement."

Moving through Longbranch, with its overlapping events, abutting fragments from various decades, interior walls scarred from earlier lives spent outdoors—the entirely of its unique social, familial, and aesthetic history—one is reminded that, however overused the word may be in architectural circles, sometimes *palimpsest* is an entirely appropriate description. And the house's next life will be its most unexpected yet: The Olsons plan to have the building and grounds transformed, after their deaths, into a retreat for creative people. "I don't want to worry about my descendants fighting over it and selling it," Olson explains. "Katherine and I just decided that it could be an inspiration for others, the way it has been for us."

And why not? It's Longbranch.

RIGHT: By 2003, the original bunkhouse had become a kitchen/ dining pavilion.
OPPOSITE: That same year, Olson added a linear volume, with a living room at one end and a bath at the other, which partly enclosed the 1959 structure.

ABOVE & BELOW: A one-story dark volume, enclosing a library, connects to the new projecting master suite.

OPPOSITE: The Olsons' bedroom opens onto a private terrace.

ABOVE & OPPOSITE:
The new master suite
continues the procession
from the existing house
through the library,
dividing the bedroom
into sleeping and
lounging zones before
terminating in the bath.

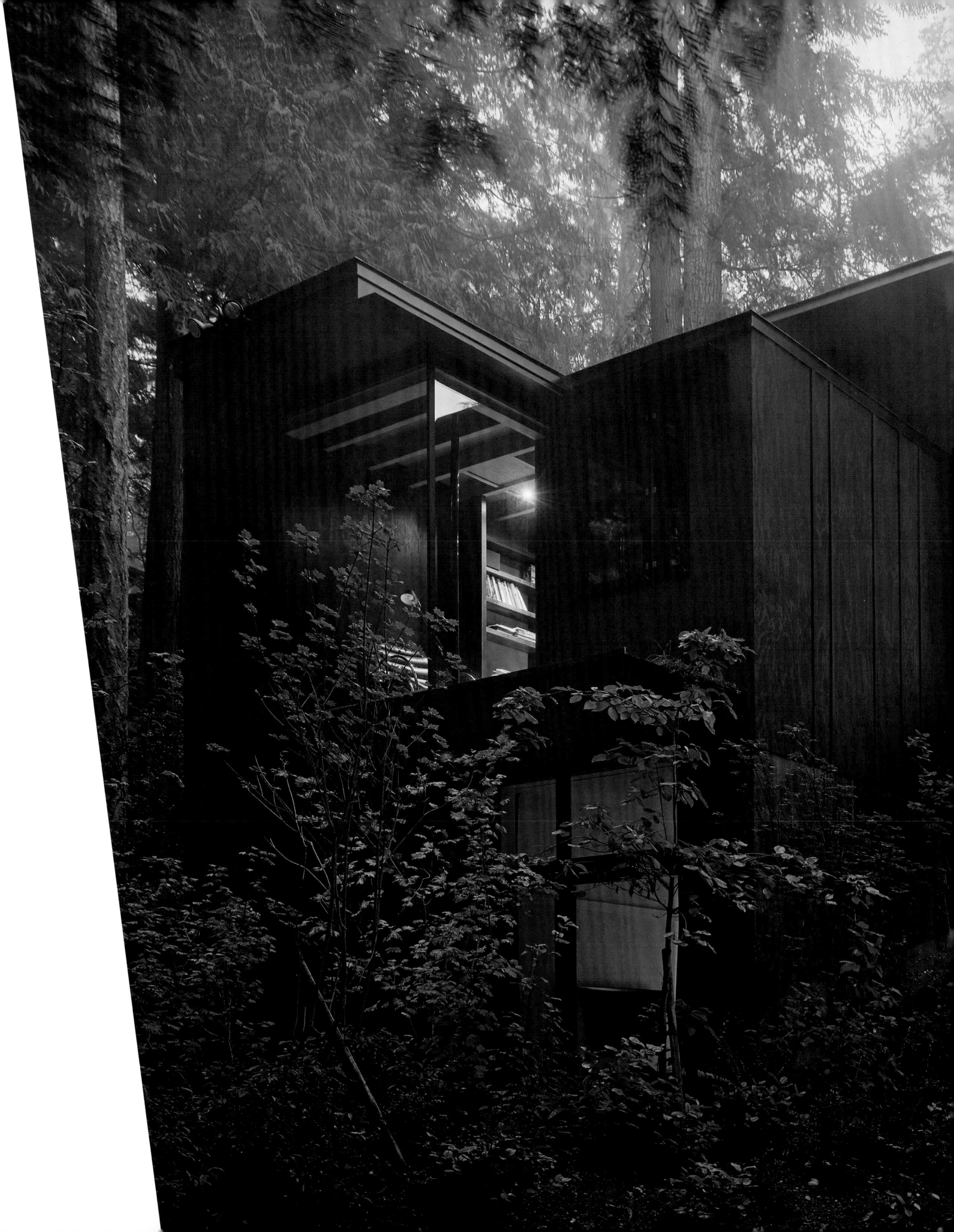

11

WAKELINS

wickhambrook, england

OPPOSITE: James
Gorst's addition to the
original lime plaster
house is finished in
custom-crafted strips
of scalloped oak.

"I DON'T LIKE BUYING THINGS NEW," SAYS Richard Morris. "It's more fun when you build."

A native Bostonian, Morris doesn't represent as a typical American Anglophile, but in fact his appreciation of the pleasures of rural England is well-schooled and discerning. Morris, a businessman, bought his first country cottage there in 1987, in a West Suffolk village called Higham, as a weekend retreat. His reasoning was impeccable. "If you go south of London, it's commuterland all the way to the Channel," Morris says. "Rural Kent was too far away. And going up north meant the M1, which was terrible even in the eighties." Suffolk, conversely, offered "empty, unfashionable country with no motorways." Morris also wanted to live near "a proper English market town," and the county's Bury St Edmunds fit the bill.

"By 2000, I figured I'd be retired in five years," Morris relates. "And I had this fantasy that I'd keep my place in London but base myself in this area." That meant a bigger property, where he and his lady friend could have parties and guests. At that point Morris's logical mind succumbed to his adventurous nature. "I wanted," he says, "a house that needed work."

He found it about ten miles southwest of Bury St Edmunds, in a village called Wickhambrook—which is, in fact, anything but empty and unfashionable. The train lets you off at Newmarket, one of the world's legendary thoroughbred racing capitals, and a misty, aromatic land of emerald green pastures, magnificent horses, and unmistakable affluence. "Most of the money is racing related, and the countryside is manicured and attractive, and there are lovely East Anglian homes," says James Gorst, Morris's architect, as he drives to the house, named Wakelins after a fifteenth-century owner.

Gorst is enthusiastic about the local residential architecture, of which Wakelins is representative. "They were built out of seasoned English oak, from about 1453 to 1650," the architect says. "It's timber frame construction, with lime plaster applied to strips of chestnut lath on the interior and exterior faces. Originally there'd have been steeply pitched thatch roofs, though generally they've been replaced with clay pegged tiles." Both the frame and the plaster offer benefits. "These timber buildings are five hundred years old and sound as a nut, because they're flexible," Gorst says. "They actually creak and move when the wind is strong, like ships. And the lime plaster breathes—it absorbs moisture but releases it as well."

Wakelins evolved over time, beginning (it is believed—dating houses, unless they're well documented, remains an uncertain science) in 1313, with a tiny, two-story cottage, to which a second more or less identical volume was later appended. The major extension took place around 1500, when "Mr. Wakelin," as Gorst calls him, "who was the manager of all the estates around here," roughly doubled the size of the building with a two-story addition. According to Morris, the three structures, though connected, weren't unified—"they remained separate dwellings, each with its own front door," he says.

"It was bought in the 1960s by an English family returning from India," Morris relates. "The work they did on the house was, I like to say, 'without benefit of clergy'—they just brought in a builder. They cut a hole in the center and put in a pine staircase—this in a building made entirely from oak—but never resolved the room patterns from the originals, so in a house that wasn't very big there were a lot of corridors."

The owners took off the thatched roof and replaced it with tile, installed metal-frame windows, and fattened the structure with a number of lean-to extensions on the rear elevation. "But the killer

blow," says Morris, "was that they replaced the exterior lime render with cement, which meant that the house couldn't breathe." By the time he discovered it, and despite the advantages—"6¼ acres, six miles south of where I used to be, and with good outbuildings"—Wakelins was, Morris had to admit, "a wreck."

Nonetheless, both owner and architect, who'd collaborated previously on Morris's London flat, were optimistic and in accord about what needed to be done. Before work could proceed, however, they had to gain the approval of the local planning authorities, as in 1974 Wakelins had received a Grade II listing, defined on the Historic England website as being "of special interest warranting every effort to preserve" it. The rules permitted Gorst to raze the lean-tos and use their square footage plus an additional twenty percent to create an addition. When he and Morris presented their plans, "the parish council, and the Suffolk historic buildings group, were both in favor," the owner says. "And then the woman who'd sold the house to me objected, and that caused a kerfuffle—my neighbor wrote a letter objecting to the difference between the proposed new wing and the old. 'Not in keeping' is the classic English phrase."

The pair ultimately prevailed in part because Gorst was "a local boy—born and brought up in Bury—and so wasn't regarded as an evil London modernist interloper, and because the council initially told James they were going to say yes and then got cold feet," Morris recalls. "Once they understood that there was a mad American willing to spend a small fortune resurrecting this wreck, they gave approval." Gorst's redesign of the existing house put the dining room, kitchen, entry hall, and music room on the ground floor, and a master suite, guest room, and TV room above, with the two connected by a stair off the entry hall at the approximate middle of the plan (a second guest room is tucked into an attic space above the master). The new wing features a living room/study below and another master suite above, with the floors linked via a secondary stair.

The architect's approach to the old structure was a mutually enriching mix of restoration and reconsideration. "We replaced fifty-five percent of the original oak timber frame—using no nails, only wooden pegs—and preserved the old exposed beams," Gorst recalls. "The two chimneys are built from Tudor-dimension bricks, which were made in a very old established brickworks in Suffolk." Rather than fireplaces ("which were never a part of the vocabulary of these houses"), ingle-nooks with wood-burning stoves were introduced. Metal lath replaced the original chestnut, but beneath the new lime plaster, the house is insulated in the traditional manner, with sheep's wool. A clay tile roof substitutes for thatch, but the handmade window glass would have been

ABOVE: The pond off the front façade is complemented by a formal reflecting pool behind the addition.

ABOVE: Gorst removed a series of shed structures from the original and restored its slender profile, which facilitates natural light and cross-ventilation.

familiar to Mr. Wakelin. "We had to restore the house," Morris says. "But wherever possible, we rebuilt with the same techniques and materials as would have been used five hundred years ago."

The removal of the lean-to extensions, moreover, returned the house to its original slender linear plan; with the exception of a short corridor off the upstairs bedrooms, the structure is essentially one room wide. Here, history meets modernity: Old houses were kept narrow to draw in sunlight throughout the day and facilitate natural ventilation, "sustainable" objectives that remain desirable and contemporary. The enfilade layout, Gorst believes, also makes the experience more interesting. "The house gets away from that awful thing you find in England, which is rooms off corridors," the architect says. "Instead of going along a dull hallway, you have what Corbusier called a *promenade architecturale*—you go on a walk through the house, with each space opening onto the next."

The new wing, which continues the house's narrow, linear character from the late medieval to the modern era, is crisply designed and carefully crafted. Yet the extension is tied firmly to the original, both tectonically and in terms of the house's narrative. "Wakelins gave me the opportunity to counterpoint late medieval timber frame construction with a modern factory-procured one," says Gorst with satisfaction. "That's how the extension's frame was made—it came along and went up in ten days." The cladding, conversely—vertical strips of bespoke scalloped oak, "each piece done in a joiner's shop to our design"—was hand-crafted and installed carefully. The outcome is a contemporary iteration of a traditional barn, rendered in a modernist language with a local flavor, and appended to the old house in a way that an outbuilding might legitimately have been in the old days. "It feels very different, and I wanted it to," says the architect. "But the closed nature of the rear elevation gives it a barnlike quality—you have something that works for today without losing the qualities of the original."

Gorst's cleverest bit of legerdemain was his response to three interconnected challenges: the need to maintain an equality of scale between the new and old wings and a desire for a high-ceilinged entertaining area on the extension's ground floor—while still keeping a stair-free connection between the structures on the upper story. The architect's solution was to set the entire extension a foot and a half below ground. "That gave you an eleven-foot ceiling height in the living room, a continuous floor level between the buildings upstairs—and the extension actually seems slightly smaller than the main house," Morris says.

If Wakelins's historic and contemporary components were united by Gorst's handling of space, the bond was further tightened by craft. Influenced by the Arts and Crafts ideal of a house as a full integration of aesthetic components, Gorst designed many of the handmade furniture pieces. He also continued the aesthetic and material language of the objects in what might be characterized as the furniture of the architecture, in particular the oak-finished partitions that lightly separate the dining room and kitchen and the sleeping and dressing areas in the "historic" master suite.

It is this "consistency of the interior language," as Morris puts it, that ultimately makes Wakelins legible as a house belonging simultaneously to the present and past. "It's a contemporary house in a historic shell, a Miesian structure built from traditional materials," Morris says. "That surprised a lot of the people who came to see it. On the outside, they'd say, well, the perfectly restored Tudor house looks a lot different from the new thing. But once they got inside,

they saw how it all made sense, there wasn't any dissonance. And because of that, you're constantly drawn from old to new and back — there's a magnetic pull in both directions."

Deciding what to lose, what to keep, and what to add remains a tricky business when dealing with historic buildings. And yet, says Gorst, "England is full of Georgian houses with Victorian extensions, Tudor houses with Queen Anne behinds—this miscegenation of styles has always happened. The difference is that people have lost confidence in contemporary architecture." There is, however, no alternative. "I've become impatient with the philosophy, in English conservation, that everything that's happened to an old house is part of the narrative," the architect admits, "because sometimes it's clear the story's taken a wrong turn, and one needs to go back and rewrite it." The trick, he adds, "is to come up with an idiom that is contextually sensitive—but all the same expresses itself as unambiguously of our time."

OPPOSITE & RIGHT:
A stair just past the entry
leads to the second floor
of the original house.
Gorst interleaved old and
new by setting an oak-
paneled enclosure with
a steel handrail opposite
the original timbered
wall. The architect
received permission to
enlarge the "protected"
historic window.

OPPOSITE & ABOVE:

The kitchen and
dining room are lightly
separated by a furniture-
like floating volume with
cabinets on one side and
a sideboard with drawers
on the other. The
new inglenook, with its
herringbone-patterned
masonry, complements
the original rough-hewn
beams and timbers.

BELOW & OPPOSITE: Past the entry inglenook, a left turn leads into the music room, where Gorst's custom-designed high-backed settee forms a "virtual" corridor. The door connects to the glazed link leading to the new living room, set three steps below ground level.

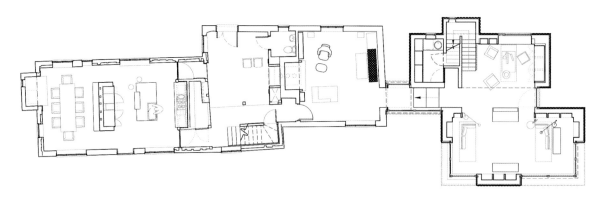

ABOVE: For the office, which adjoins the living room's sitting area (PREVIOUS PAGE, BOTTOM), Gorst designed a custom-crafted desk in sympathy with the architecture.

ABOVE: On the addition's second floor, the master suite is surfaced in book-matched walnut—"Luxury without ostentation," says Gorst. The beams abstract the rough timbers in the original house.

12
COLLAGE HOUSE
london, england

"IT'S AN INTERESTING COMMUNITY HERE," says architect Jonathan Tuckey of his stretch of Kilburn Lane, just south of Queen's Park in northwest London. "It's quite busy; buses go up and down, and it's anonymous—the kind of road where you don't know who lives on it." And yet, despite the unremarkable storefronts and solid brick architecture, Tuckey adds, "the area isn't as introspective as the façades make it seem."

Or as straightforward. Though Kilburn Lane is aggressively urban today, "there was not much on the map here that wasn't farm until the late 1840s and 1850s," Tuckey says. "Notting Hill, farther south, had happened, and the network of streets directly southwest of here, which were built up for railway workers, was architecturally quite interesting." Tuckey's house, and its neighbors, were developed to provide services to the residential blocks. "On the maps, they were described as 'works,'" he says. "Our building was a laundry, as was the neighboring one. Or they were light-industrial, with the janitor or head foreman in a flat upstairs."

A hundred years later, the architect explains, "The commercial occupation of quite a few of these had disappeared, and the ground floors had been boarded up, though people were still living upstairs." Tuckey's building remained an exception, though the laundry had long since decamped and been replaced by a steel fabricator specializing in kitchen worktops. "The business occupied the whole property—the ground floor was a workshop, the upstairs an office, and the top floor was a store."

Along with the "works," whatever charms the environs might have conveyed had also mostly decamped. "When we first got here, I thought, forget it, I don't want to live on this street, with smashed cars all over," Tuckey remembers. Then he peeked through a hole in the

OPPOSITE: To maximize space and natural light in his long and narrow, nearly windowless London home, Jonathan Tuckey opened up existing skylights, created new ones, and eliminated corridors in favor of an enfilade plan.

roller shutter covering part of the ground floor façade, and his architect's instincts kicked in. "You could see down this narrow alley of metalwork into darkness. And I had a feeling this could be quite exciting."

What Tuckey discovered when he gained access to what proved to be a long and narrow L-shaped property—the original house in front and a series of later shed structures behind it—calls to mind an industrial-strength version of Samuel Beckett. "There were three workers who didn't communicate with one another, and they each had their own rooms and were surrounded by what looked like about seventy years' worth of accumulated stuff. And then there was one guy in the office, so there's four people in 3,500 square feet of junk." Despite knowing the dimensions, Tuckey believed the property was in fact smaller because "you couldn't see the walls. And then you got to the end, and sort of shined a torch into the darkness."

Tuckey's purchase agreement stipulated that the property had to be delivered empty, and when he and his wife first saw the denuded space, they were thunderstruck. "It was extraordinary to see how expansive it was," the architect admits. "We had bought more space than we could afford to build," Tuckey says. "Suddenly, we had to be very economical in how we approached this." In his practice, Tuckey tells clients who've purchased old buildings to spend as much time in them as possible before finalizing the program, and he took his own advice, moving his practice into the building's second floor and waiting a year before putting pen to paper. "The brief was developed in lots of conversations about how we wanted to live," the architect recalls.

Ironically, despite all the talking and thinking (not to mention professional expertise), he almost got it wrong. The initial plan put the main living area on the first floor of the house, with bedrooms for

experience—you'd be constantly walking down this long, dark tube." Instead, Tuckey's lightly divided procession of spaces maximizes the structure's full width, draws in natural illumination from above, and offers an unobstructed view virtually from the front door to the garden's back wall.

The plan's overall legibility, however, did not prevent Tuckey from investing it with considerable surprise. The first beat in the procession, the low-ceilinged prelude to the living room, features a door leading to what Tuckey describes as "a combination attic and toilet." The room introduces a number of motifs, not least the architect's simultaneous attraction to propriety and unconventionality. "I was upset that we didn't have a proper attic, where friends can rifle through wedding presents and CDs," Tuckey explains. At the same time, "We didn't want a powder room that is neat and tidy." Accordingly, Tuckey set the visitors' WC in an oversize storage closet stacked to the ceiling with stuff—"you sit down, and you're surrounded by absolutely everything on display."

The closet walls are composed of exposed wood studs set against beech plywood—as opposed to finished Sheetrock—an idea that continues throughout the house. "We wanted to do something beautiful without adornment, and thought the proportions and rhythm of the studs would be quite nice," the architect says. "It was our way of expressing the elegance of ordinary construction."

The low-ceilinged zone gives way to the living room, half of which rises into a twenty-three-foot-high, skylit space; a mezzanine-level office sits atop the living room's other side and keeps it cozy. A floating wood "box" with seating and shelf space screens the area from the kitchen/dining room beyond—"otherwise it would have been too much view of the garden," the architect says. Interestingly, Tuckey continued the exposed-stud wall motif in the living room, then took it a step further, creating a simple stud screen to enclose the stair leading up to the mezzanine—a "virtual" wall that leaves the stair entirely on view. In addition to keeping the narrow space from feeling smaller, the architect's screen also encourages play. "Our children and their friends are constantly diving between the studs and onto the sofa," he says. "It's amazingly appealing to them."

With its peaked roof crowned by a long skylight, exposed beams and trusses, and brick walls still bearing the painted notations of workmen—and the wall-size glass doors opening onto the garden—the dining/kitchen pavilion, sited in the sole surviving shed, is the residence's standout spot. Though it seems only lightly touched, Tuckey in fact did considerable work in the pavilion, exposing the skylight and restoring the roof studs, removing a divider that split the space in two, relocating one of the "bowstring" trusses, and shortening the entire structure to make more room for the garden.

the Tuckeys and their two young daughters on the levels above; the kitchen and dining area in the adjacent shed behind it; then a garden replacing the remaining derelict structures; and, in the L's short leg, a new single-story structure for the architect's office. To Tuckey, it made perfect sense. "At the time, I had one guy on staff. And it was obvious—he'd come in every morning, we'd have a cup of coffee, and then go back through the garden and to work," he says.

Then one day, Tuckey's employee pointed out what in retrospect seems glaringly obvious: that as the practice grew, he'd be adding staff, so eventually he might have half a dozen architects traipsing through his house all day. Why not reverse the program, and put the office upstairs in front (accessible via a public stair), and the bedrooms overlooking the garden in the rear? "It was a revelation," Tuckey says. "Why would you want to open your bedroom window onto the street when you could sleep in peace on a courtyard?" Tuckey changed the plan, setting the office in a four-hundred-square-foot space over the living room, and a duplex rental apartment above it, and relocating the bedrooms to the back (when his practice eventually outgrew the at-home studio, he converted it to a second rental apartment).

One of Tuckey's first design decisions involved eliminating a circulation corridor from the plan and having the rooms between the entrance and the garden open directly onto one another. This grew out of the constraints of the site: It was only sixteen feet wide, without the possibility of windows on either side, and with a length of roughly 115 feet. "A corridor would have produced an absolutely miserable

ABOVE & OPPOSITE: Tuckey eliminated the derelict sheds in the short leg of his L-shaped property and replaced them with a garden and new two-story bedroom wing.

Certain design flourishes seem as though they could have been part of the room's original language, notably the elegantly shaped, slender copper pipes that deliver water to the sink (and repeat in the powder room and master bath), and the long metal counter, enameled by the company that makes signage for the London Underground. At the room's far end, by the dining area and garden entrance, a raised floor and dropped ceiling, spanned by another of Tuckey's stud screens, forms the bridge to the domestic wing. "It prepares you for the slightly lower ceiling that pervades the sleeping area," Tuckey says, "and the screen suggests the end of the house's public part."

The bedroom wing, a simple, two-story glass-and-wood box, sited at the garden's rear and accessed from the kitchen via a short hallway, remains the house's only completely new element. Yet the site's history has found its way into Tuckey's scheme, notably in the mammoth tiled family bath, which sits fully, immodestly exposed to its surroundings at the end of the hall. With its robust copper pipes and wash basin, and sloped countertop terminating above an open drain trough, the bath resembles a cross between a commercial laundry and a boiler room—both of which reference the once light-industrial character of the neighborhood and the building's original function. The family-size tub reflects the district's Turkish baths, which the Tuckeys used to frequent. Indicating the three copper pipes, thick as a church organ's, that fill the tub, he describes the family ritual: "These boiler pipes fill it up really fast, and it gets very, very hot, and then we run out to the little pool in the garden, which is very, very cold. We do that year-round."

The ways in which Tuckey's house connects to its surroundings also straddle the present day and history. On the one hand, his relationship with his neighbors represents a twenty-first-century, west London exercise in community. "All of our houses overlook one another around what is essentially a big courtyard," the architect says, standing on the roof and indicating the buildings to the west. "One old guy restores all the church organs in the south of England. Then there's five or six recording studios—there's always bands on the rooftops, chatting through the night."

Rather than encroaching on one another's turf, says Tuckey, "we all look out for one another in quite a nice way," and the house's design encourages the connection. "Our neighbor's daughter is thirteen, and for five years she's been forgetting her keys, so she comes through here and goes over the roof to her back door," he says. "I love that. I love it that, if the musicians are making too much noise, we can ask them to quiet down. It's a good balance, and if we'd all enforced the usual privacy expectations, we would have shut down those possibilities."

ABOVE & OPPOSITE: Past the nondescript front door, Tuckey's residence opens into a low-ceilinged entry hall leading to a 23-foot-high skylit living room partially covered by a mezzanine. The powder room, which doubles as an attic, is just past the front door.

TWELVE COLLAGE HOUSE

179

Yet it is a contemporary way of living that draws on the memory of the site, of an industrial era when privacy was the privilege of the rich, people lived and worked in one another's faces, and indeed, took to the skies. "There are descriptions in Samuel Pepys's diaries of people getting exercise on the roofs, walking the leads and flashings because the air down below was so much dirtier," Tuckey says. "It wasn't until the twentieth century that the front door was the only way in and out, and the roofs were for keeping the water off."

Interleaving old and new, the architect believes, offers benefits both practical and philosophical. "Starting with an empty lot is much more terrifying as a creative proposition," he explains. "Whereas collaborating with something that preexists generates a series of constraints, which I really like. It allows you to investigate what a building might have been, to pull out parts and try to find things you like and don't like." It also enriches a project's narrative. "You've already got a story, and you're adding another layer to it," Tuckey says. "The laundry into metal workshop into residence—I think this would have been a much more shallow project if it were just a house on a plot of land. Narrative is really important to me—the sense of being part of a continuum." Tuckey's collaboration with history includes not only what preceded him but that which his family has created. "I think of buildings as being responsive to the ways people occupy them, and the house has evolved under our stewardship. That's why old and new will always sit together, and why I like to celebrate it in how we do our work."

One part of the house's history has thus far resisted revision: the previous owner's façade, with its sign advertising custom metalwork, which the Tuckeys left in place. "We can't quite work out what to do yet," the architect admits—"I occasionally get people ringing our doorbell asking for a kitchen." This is, however, less a failure of imagination on the architect's part than curiosity about what the future holds. "When we bought it, there was quite a lot of sentimentalizing of turn-of-the-century industrial signage. And I'm fascinated to discover whether or not a Perspex sign with vinyl lettering will ever become something people find beautiful. Hopefully," he adds, "I'll live long enough to find out."

OPPOSITE & RIGHT: The living room fireplace continues up and beyond the skylight in the soaring space, increasing the sense of height. The mezzanine serves as a study.

FOLLOWING SPREAD: The kitchen/dining area, in a preexisting shed, preserves the character of the original and many of its structural elements. A passageway, beside the glass doors, leads to the house's domestic wing.

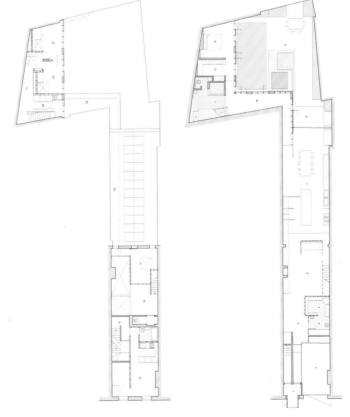

LEFT & OPPOSITE: Tuckey added sympathetic new features to the kitchen, notably exposed copper piping. A water channel, connecting to a pool in the garden, is fed from a tap by the dining table.

OPPOSITE & BELOW: An L-shaped corridor leads from the kitchen/dining shed into the two-story bedroom wing. At the L's bend is the fully exposed bath. "I liked the idea of it being *uber*, like the power room of a ship," Tuckey says. A copper basin stands in for a sink—"you fill it up, then tip the water down the sloped counter into a drain."

LEFT: The Tuckeys use
the water feature in the
garden as a cold plunge
after taking hot baths.

13

California: Historic Modernism

SHULMAN HOUSE

los angeles

+

IKE HOUSE

san diego

OPPOSITE: Julius Shulman's house (ABOVE), designed by Raphael Soriano, is an LA landmark. The John Ike residence (BELOW) was built by a naval officer using enlisted men as labor.

LIKE "JUMBO SHRIMP," THE PHRASE "HISTORIC modernism" is one of those oxymorons that rarely receives consideration. Partly this has to do with the fact that, though modern architecture in its many iterations has been around for more than a century, it is still seen as somehow less worthy of serious consideration—less genuine or authentic—than the classical kind. This is true even among those who should know better. One would assume that architects themselves would see modernism as part of the continuum of their profession. Yet I have had conversations with major practitioners (usually specializing in shingle style or Greek and Colonial Revival residential work) who believe that only those who'd been (as one put it to me) "brainwashed" by the dons of the northeast-architecture-school mafia could possibly think that a rectilinear glass and steel composition was anything other than tectonic snake oil.

Given the surprising prevalence of this attitude among those who actually make architecture, it should come as no surprise that there are still places in America where you cannot get a bank loan to build a house with a flat roof. Like psychiatry, another established, influential fact of life that is still (more than one hundred fifty years after the birth of Freud) looked upon with suspicion (even by psychiatrists), modernist architecture is widely regarded as something to which only the gullible or pretentious, or those who've lost touch with life's fundamental values, could possibly be susceptible.

Yet modernism is indeed an historic movement—one that is increasingly seen as worthy of preservation. In and around New Canaan, Connecticut, for example, midcentury homes by the so-called Harvard Five, the most famous of whom were Philip Johnson and Marcel Breuer, and other likeminded architects, have been landmarked, protected, and creatively restored, expanded, and reinterpreted. Perhaps nowhere is this impulse more prevalent than in southern California, home of the Case Study Houses program, which spawned, between 1945 and 1966, twenty-four residences that drew on the vocabulary and spirit of modernism to create templates for inexpensive, livable single-family homes. Today, many of these projects, by such blue-chip names as Eames, Saarinen, and Neutra, are as sought-after and fetishized as Fabergé eggs—Pierre Koenig's 1959 Stahl House, in particular, has served as the backdrop for countless photo shoots and is regarded as the acme of cool, an architectural Steve McQueen.

But the Case Study projects and other West Coast midcentury modern residences, which combine European and Japanese influences, the Mediterranean tradition of indoor/outdoor living, and the industrial know-how developed by the wartime defense industry, amount to more than the right stuff; they were envisioned as a valu-

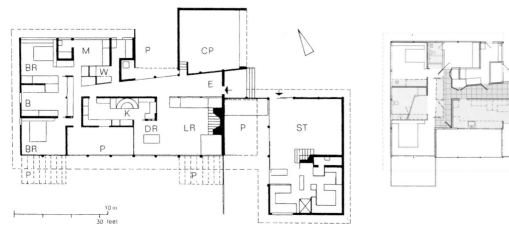

BR
M
P
CP
W
B
E
K
DR
LR
P
ST
BR
P
P
P

10 m
30 feet

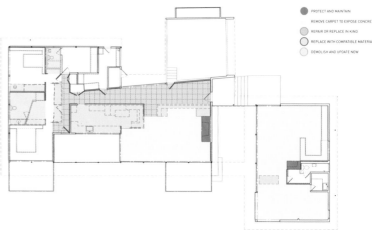

PROTECT AND MAINTAIN

REMOVE CARPET TO EXPOSE CONCRETE

REPAIR OR REPLACE IN KIND

REPLACE WITH COMPATIBLE MATERIAL

DEMOLISH AND UPDATE NEW

able solution to the postwar housing shortage, and expressed the liberal democratic philosophy of the New Deal (to which many of the era's seminal architects subscribed). As such, southern California's residential modernism stands as a movement of high political, social, and industrial—as well as architectural—importance: history-making in every sense.

Making such homes new again—sustaining their essence while rendering them suitable for twenty-first-century habitation—is trickier than one might imagine, given that they're "modern." As these two projects suggest, success lies in balancing a house's program not only with the particulars of preservation and the pull of style but an awareness of midcentury modernism's enduring cultural significance—especially in California, land of opportunity and self-reinvention.

By 1947, Julius Shulman had become a highly successful architecture photographer and, though he'd taken but one of the two pictures (of the Kaufmann and Stahl Houses) that solidified his position as perhaps the greatest practitioner of the genre, had demonstrated a special affinity for—and ability to showcase—California's modernist residences. Strongly associated with Richard Neutra, who'd given him his start, when it came time to build his own house, on a two-acre Laurel Canyon property for which he paid $2,500, Shulman instead turned to Raphael Soriano, a Sephardic Jewish immigrant from Rhodes who'd been Neutra's assistant before starting his own practice. When I met the photographer in 2007, he cited personal reasons for his choice—"Neutra was a nice guy, pleasant, a gentleman, but not warm and spirited like Soriano, with his Mediterranean background"—but budget and, especially, the ability to have input also affected his decision.

Still, Soriano was no pushover and, though lesser known today than other of the Case Study participants, proved an innovative, forward-thinking practitioner. "Soriano was interested in a cohesive building philosophy for the twentieth century," observed his biographer Wolfgang Wagener, and in fact his investigations into prefab buildings and the promise of plan-freeing steel frame construction were far ahead of their time. The architect was seeking clients who'd let him test his theories, and with Shulman, a friend and fellow creator, he had one. They signed a contract for a four-thousand-square-foot, three-bedroom home and studio—"$40,000, all cash," Shulman recalled—and Soriano went to work.

Soriano's plan put the house on an east-west axis, with the public rooms set against a tapering gallery that led from the front door to the bedrooms; the living and dining rooms and master suite faced south across the lawn and captured the sunlight and spectacular canyon and mountain views. "The Shulmans helped contribute as much to the performance of the house as myself," the architect observed, and indeed it would be hard to imagine a better-informed client. Having photographed dozens of modernist houses, and wanting to enlighten the public regarding their potential—one of his great innovations, the placement of people in domestic scenarios within his pictures, was meant specifically to show how the houses could be enjoyed—Shulman understood both their strengths and shortcomings. "I knew from experience that most people didn't use their sliding glass doors very often, because if there were children, they'd leave them open and bugs and lizards would come in," Shulman told me. Accordingly, he requested that Soriano add screen porches on the south side, to create habitable volumes that cut the wind and solar glare, kept the pests out, and, he later wrote, created "a feeling of enclosure that psychologically as well as visually conveys comfort and protection." Initially, the architect resisted. "He was a bachelor, he didn't know about family living," Shulman recalled. But Soriano acquiesced, and the translucent porches, which elegantly bridge indoor and outdoor space, became the house's signature.

The architect did install one of his first steel frames—which in Shulman's in-progress photos appears as a simple post-and-beam design—to great effect. Shortly after the photographer, his wife, and their four-year-old daughter moved in, in March of 1950, the house was hit by an earthquake-induced landslide. According to Wagener, "Tons of rock and debris plunged through the service patio and the gallery into the living room." Shulman broke his leg—but the steel frame was undamaged, and the plaster of the ceiling didn't even crack.

When Shulman invited me to the house, to profile him for a magazine, he was ninety-six years old and had been in residence for fifty-seven years. Yet his pride in the place remained undiminished. "It's very simple. Three bedrooms, two bathrooms," he said, giving me the tour. "It's not a house with eighteen bedrooms and twenty-five bathrooms, like you see advertised in the papers." The cork-lined entry hall, hung with his photographs, was entirely original—"it's a wonderful material, no maintenance"—and the pocket door leading to his bedroom still worked perfectly: "The carpenters assumed we'd have a six-foot, eight-inch door with a transom, but Soriano told them to build it into the frame, and they did a good job." He was especially pleased with the property, which he'd first explored as a Boy Scout in the 1920s. "I knew the hills were wild because the Scout camp had been here," Shulman said as we made our

OPPOSITE: Landscape architect Mia Lehrer kept signature elements of "Julius's jungle," but echoed the architecture with a series of Cor-Ten in-ground planters that zone the property and separate it from the canyon.

way through the overgrown garden he referred to as "Julius's Jungle." "We're at 1,300 feet elevation here," he reported. "Fresh, clean air. Behind this is fifty-three more acres belonging to the Santa Monica Conservancy"—adding, with satisfaction, "Forever land."

In fact, Shulman radiated satisfaction as he pushed the walker he called "the Mercedes" around the house and studio, and spoke of his accomplishments in a way that was at once egomaniacal and self-kidding. "I'm always identified as being the best architectural photographer in the world," he confided with amusement. "But I disclaim that—I say, 'One of the best.'" Shulman had become a landmark—and so, in 1987, had the house. One of only twelve remaining Soriano projects, and the only one with an unaltered steel frame, it had been designated a Los Angeles Historic-Cultural Monument.

"My daughter will never sell the place, and her son will probably live here when he grows up—he's only twenty-five or thirty now," the photographer joked as I left. But after Shulman's

death in 2009, the house went on the market. It proved a hard sell. "It was available for well over a year and had been in escrow twice," says the new owner, who purchased the place with his wife. "The family discovered that the buyers wanted to make dramatic changes," which would have violated both its landmark status and design integrity. "We loved it as it was," he says.

Perhaps. But the place remained, after nearly sixty years, virtually unchanged, down to Shulman's beloved shag carpet, and was badly in need of restoration. And though the couple had no children at the time (they now have two), they wanted—as had the Shulmans—a house that would support the needs and aspirations of a young family. When the pair engaged Los Angeles architect Lorcan O'Herlihy to work with them, the mandate was not only to modernize the structure and reinterpret certain of its elements in a contemporary idiom, but to bring the house into the twenty-first century while maintaining the spirit of daily renewal that had sustained Shulman and his family.

Knowing that any work would be governed by the LA Office of Historic Resources preservation guidelines, "We did extensive research into the building and finishing materials, and Soriano's design intentions," O'Herlihy explains. Fortunately for the architect and his

ABOVE & OPPOSITE: In Shulman's studio, separated from the main house by a small garden, O'Herlihy kept the layout and essential elements while updating the materials and functions. Curtains were replaced by screens, which enhance the architecture's layered character.

THE NEW OLD HOUSE

LEFT & OPPOSITE: The house's screened zones were Shulman's idea, and enabled the photographer and his family to enjoy the outdoors while also being protected from it.

clients, Lambert Giessinger, the Office's historic preservation architect, was receptive to the idea of the residence as what O'Herlihy calls "a living organism. Lambert took the position that these houses should keep the elements that establish their landmark status but have the ability to change over time—to have an ongoing life." "It could have gone in the direction of being the Julius Shulman House Museum, but then you couldn't have had a family in it," Giessinger affirms. "The more important question is, if we brought back Shulman, would he recognize the project as his, and I think the answer is yes—not that we're using a Ouija board."

O'Herlihy established his own guidelines, which influenced the project at different scales. The house's defining elements—its exterior materials and colors, the screen porches, the cork-lined entry hall—were preserved. When finishes required replacement, the same ones were specified. The plumbing and electrical systems required contemporization, and certain elements, like the original radiant-heat system embedded in the concrete floor slab, were beyond reclamation; ultimately, O'Herlihy concealed individual HVAC units in all the rooms, which facilitates bespoke temperature control and saved the architect from having to put an unsightly machine on the roof. But in all respects, the old is perceptible within the new. "We redid the kitchen, but kept the lines; the cabinetry is identical in its proportions; the windows are where they should be," O'Herlihy says by way of example. "Sometimes, as an architect, what you *don't* do is as important as what you do."

Ultimately, each of the house's elements and areas became a mediation between history and modernity. The screen porches were refurbished, and the original heavy drapes replaced throughout with a series of "screening veils" that filter the light and reinforce the architecture's layered, planar character. Carpets were removed and a new coating of polished, patinated concrete added to the original slab. Shulman's studio was transformed into an office and guest quarters; the photographer's storage closets were replaced with bookshelves and cabinetry; the original bathroom was converted to a clothes closet and a new one installed.

In the circulation gallery, says the owner, "The city allowed us to buy the exact same cork tiles from the exact same manufacturer, which quickly weathered to look like the old ones." O'Herlihy added a skylight at the approximate midpoint, brightening what had been a dark corridor. Shulman and Soriano had lightly separated the entry gallery from the living room with a three-quarter height millwork volume that incorporated indirect lighting, shelves, and seating ("That was my doing," Shulman told me. "In the original plans that element went up to the ceiling."); O'Herlihy replaced it with a more streamlined version, finished like the original in Douglas fir, with a long cantilevered bench.

The one place where architect and owners altered the plan—and only very slightly—was in the domestic zone. At some point, the Shulmans had made the master bath smaller, converting part of the space into what appeared to be a lady's dressing area, with a

vanity table and seat, that was effectively part of the hallway running between the bedrooms. Using Soriano's original plan to justify the change to Giessinger, O'Herlihy returned the dressing area to the enlarged and redesigned bath.

Los Angeles has an exceptionally rich lode of important residential architecture, representing multiple periods and styles. And while much of O'Herlihy's practice in cities (LA included) involves multi-unit infill projects at a larger scale, his office remains committed to the idea of "amplified urbanism"—elevating the conditions surrounding a given project, acting as a catalyst—even on stand-alone residences such as Shulman's. "This house is part of the historic fabric of the city, an infill project of a different sort," the architect observes. "Midcentury modernism is an important part of the overall context, an enormous legacy. And it elevates everything to be able to see that."

Showing me the studio, the owner opens a door to reveal an astonishing sight: Shulman's original, unrenovated darkroom, a surprisingly tiny space from which emerged one of the great photographic oeuvres of the twentieth century. "The city didn't tell us what to do with it," he says. "So we preserved it as a monument." The darkroom is a poignant reminder that Shulman never considered himself an artist, but rather "an at-home photographer"—one who relied upon that home to sustain the life that enabled the work. "Our house seems to accelerate in spirit and excitement as the years pass by," Shulman wrote to Soriano in 1978; twenty years later, in an introduction to one of his books, the photographer praised "Soriano's sensitivity and ability to create what today is our heaven of a glorious life." Things have changed, but the glorious life remains. As Giessinger suggests, were Shulman to return, he'd recognize the house as his own.

OPPOSITE & ABOVE: O'Herlihy preserved the living room's existing fireplace and replaced the three-quarter wall separating it from the entry gallery with a more streamlined version finished, like the original, in Douglas fir.

THIS PAGE & OPPOSITE:
Soriano's steel-frame
construction proved its
mettle when a landslide
crashed through the
gallery into the living
room shortly after the
Shulmans moved in.
O'Herlihy replaced the
original cork tiles with
identical new ones and
added a skylight.

NO AIR OF THE SACRED HANGS OVER THE VACATION home of architect John Ike. His four-bedroom, two-story clapboard residence sits atop an east-facing slope at the southern end of Point Loma, the peninsula of land that encloses San Diego Bay; the neighborhood, called Fleet Ridge (presumably in deference to Naval Base San Diego, homeport of the Pacific Fleet), was built up during and after World War II. Ike's house dates from the mid-1940s, and if there was an architect, the name has been lost to posterity; more than likely, the structure was figured out by its owner, a lieutenant commander who built it, Ike speculates, "with Seabees he'd co-opted off the base, as there wasn't a straight line in the entire place."

Yet for a one-off by an amateur, the structure had qualities Ike found seductive, primarily on the main, upper floor. The layout was felicitous, with a long circulation hall running nearly the full length of the building from north to south, with a kitchen pavilion, entry, and master suite on the street-facing side, and the living/dining room and a second bedroom across the hall overlooking the property's steeply down-sloping yard and the bay view. For a reason that neither Ike nor his consultants could determine, the kitchen and bedroom wings and hall were flat-roofed, "and then there was a sep-

arate, pitched roof plane over the living room that went down toward the hillside," Ike recalls. "Though it wasn't a pedigree house, it was interesting. A true composition, in both plan and section."

It was also a mess. "Literally, it was like they'd gone to a salvage yard and picked up old windows and doors, and threw 'em in wherever they wanted," says Ike. Other than a brick patio by the front door and a small yard by the kitchen, "there was no real outdoor space, except for a deck in back on the lower level." And whereas the main floor conveyed consideration and creativity, the downstairs was an afterthought. "There was a space behind the garage with a floor where the concrete had been poured over the dirt," the architect recalls. "It had been used as a laundry room, but there was no drain—the washing machine hose just went out into the backyard."

If it wasn't a house in which one might have expected an architect to be interested, it's true as well that Ike himself confounds expectation. A tall and portly Midwesterner with a loud, droll speaking voice, his New York–based firm, Ike Kligerman Barkley, is best known for

ABOVE & OPPOSITE: John Ike enhanced the house's existing materiality with a cork floor, and fenestrated the front hallway to bring in more light. The front door's "dinner plate" windows are original.

OPPOSITE & ABOVE:
Rather than
furnishing the house
with recognizable
midcentury classics
from Herman Miller

and Knoll, Ike's affinity
for Scandinavian
modernism led him
to design rooms "in
which the architectural

and decorative styles
don't quite match." The
Regency-Meets-Danish-
Modern dining table is
by Frits Henningsen.

THIS PAGE & OPPOSITE: Ike flattened and raised the living room roof and added bands of operable clerestory windows on both sides for cross-ventilation. The new deck is precisely the width of the room.

traditional shingle-style residences. Yet he has created a number of projects in a modernist idiom and remains a particular aficionado of hand-crafted twentieth-century Scandinavian furniture and textiles. A great fan of bold colors and vintage kitsch, Ike also loves to decorate, though, as he puts it, "I don't have the right persona. People are always surprised—'That frumpy, middle-aged guy does the interiors?'"

In fact, Ike's off-center perspective enabled him to draw a connection between his firm's signature work and California's midcentury residences. Shingle architecture, he notes, was defined as much by an opportunistic design methodology as its primary building material. "An eccentrically massed composition," Ike has written of the style's picturesque character, "may be a response to existing conditions, budget constraints, a project's changing circumstances, and/or artistic inspiration"—a "compositional freedom" that also characterized the work of the West Coast modernists. "What Rudolf Schindler did was in the shingle-style tradition," Ike observes. "There were plans and elevations, but then he'd get out there in the field and do the framing himself. And he was riffing on, *Oh, I've got this leftover piece of plywood, so maybe I can do this wall differently.* Remember," Ike adds, regarding the hous-

ing shortage that drove the Case Study program, "many of these architects' clients had no money—they were artistic servicemen."

Like a suitor who endows his beloved with qualities not evident to those whom Cupid's arrow has missed, Ike filtered the Plain-Jane house through his professional eye and saw Architecture. "If you took off your glasses and squinted at it from fifty yards away, it looked vaguely like a project by William Wurster," Ike says, citing the influential Bay Area–based practitioner and longtime dean of the UC Berkeley architecture school. Specifically, Ike had in mind Wurster's 1935 Miller House in Carmel, a "small, economical residence that was made to feel large by view-embracing expanses of glass, the use of outdoor porches and brick terracing, and the incorporation of a single material—stone-rubbed white pine boards—into all of the ceilings and walls."

This vision, and Ike's programmatic requirements, compelled the architect to move the house both backward and forward in time: to, on the one hand, make it a credible example of midcentury modern design at its most elegant (a kind of architectural Pygmalion), and then to, in effect, update his own historic restoration, by giving the house characteristics that define twenty-first-century living.

The Wurster model, it transpired, was well suited to Ike's intentions. "The architects of the California midcentury house tended to fall into one of two camps—they were either Wrightians or Miesians," he explains. "Disciples of Wright, like Schindler, favored low-slung wood architecture, very textural, and somewhat picturesque massing. Whereas the Miesians, like Neutra and Craig Ellwood, had more of the European rigor we associate with glass and steel." Wurster was an ideal point of reference, Ike believes, "because he straddled both camps—his was a softer kind of Miesian design."

As it happened, "a lot of disciples of Wright settled in San Diego, and his influence turns up a lot," says the architect—including, whether by accident or design, in the lieutenant commander's "warm and woodsy" residence. Accordingly, Ike emphasized materiality in his renovation, notably through the extensive use of cork, not only on floors but also ceilings and the bath and kitch-

ABOVE: Ike designed the rainbow-striped glass lamp beside the bar with Irene Mamiye. OPPOSITE: Both the floor and the ceiling in the kitchen are finished in cork, a sound-absorptive material that is also easy on the feet.

en counters—a finish popular at midcentury that also enabled Ike to achieve a Wurster-like monolithic materiality—as well as emphasizing texture via exposed brick, wood, and grass cloth and woven straw in the bedrooms and hallways (in a nod to his home team, Ike covered the living room walls in cedar shingles).

At the same time, the Miesian camp affected the house's most striking feature: the wall of full-height lift-and-slide glass doors that runs nearly the whole thirty-five-foot length of the living room. Gently nudging the house into more of a modernist glass pavilion informed many of Ike's design moves: He raised and flattened the living room roof, added bands of operable clerestories on both sides of the space that naturally ventilate the entire residence, replaced the solid hallway wall with translucent glass, and refenestrated the bedrooms.

"But the real bridge between the old and new," Ike believes, "is the outdoor decking," which spans the house on the view elevation on both the upper and lower floors—indeed, both the living room and its corresponding deck are fourteen feet deep, which actually as well as psychologically doubles the size of what is genuinely an in-

door/outdoor room. "Except for people like Schindler, who emphasized the continuity of interior and exterior experience, that wasn't the way folks lived in 1945," Ike says, a view reinforced by Julius Shulman's observation that people tended to keep their sliding glass doors closed. Ike's desire to open up his house benefited from the fact that Point Loma isn't terribly buggy. But it is also the case that, in the twenty-first century, dematerializing the distinction between a home and its surroundings is more of an accepted, in fact desirable, residential model. Ike's inclusion not only of the decks but of sitting and dining patios on the house's street side—with no greater nod to privacy than a low cinder-block wall—gives a modern overlay to a residence otherwise firmly anchored in the past.

The outcome is unclassifiable, temporally as well as aesthetically. If the architecture time-travels from 1935 to 2015, the flavor is somehow that of a late-sixties Lee Marvin caper film; standing on the upper deck, one can almost see the big man there, his flat affect amped to the max as he takes in the sunbaked panorama and gives laconic instructions to the twitchy thugs he's recruited for the heist. If this sounds fanciful, it is not, in fact, an association from which Ike

runs away. "I didn't have the movies in mind when I did this project," he says. "But it's almost impossible not to think scenographically when you work in houses like this in California"—or the strong relationship, one codified by Julius Shulman's photography, between midcentury architecture and narrative. Recalling the John Lautner residence in which the fashion designer Tom Ford located his LA film *A Single Man*, Ike says, "You think of these houses as stage sets."

One is a landmark, the other a quotidian example of a vernacular style. Yet both the Shulman and Ike houses tell a similar, indeed iconic, California story: that of possibility. And if it was particularly strong in those optimistic postwar years, the story still unites the past and present in our time, as Ike's experience demonstrates. "Neutra and Schindler left Europe, went out west, and did their own thing," he says. "In California, it's a loner kind of attitude, and that's the way I am, too—I'm not in fashion. Back east, I might be looking over my shoulder, wondering what everyone else thought. But out here, I'm like those other guys. I'm free."

PRECEDING SPREAD:
Ike indulged his love of
pattern and color in the
baths and downstairs
sitting room.

OPPOSITE & ABOVE:
On the house's "view"
elevation, Ike added
upper and lower decks
and a hot tub, and
planted the newly
terraced, downsloping
backyard with olive
trees.

14
SALLICK HOUSE
danbury, connecticut

OPPOSITE: Based on the plans of two Colonial houses, Barbara and Robert Sallick's home combines historic elements—including the front door, its frame, and the stone stoop—with new construction.

THE YEAR 1968 WAS ESPECIALLY TUMULTUOUS worldwide and, it could be argued, one of the very worst of the American Century. Martin Luther King Jr. was assassinated in April, and Robert Kennedy followed him to the grave two months later. In August, police clubbed antiwar demonstrators bloody on the Chicago streets outside the Democratic National Convention. In November, Richard Nixon won the presidency.

And Barbara and Robert Sallick, respectively a schoolteacher and a plumbing-supply salesman, moved into their newly finished home in Danbury, Connecticut, with their eight-month-old and a boy that was nearly four. The residence—"when all of our friends were into Danish Modern," Barbara recalls—was Colonial in style and furnished with their beloved in-period antiques.

At a glance, the young family might have seemed, in that year before Woodstock, wildly out of step with their times. In fact, as the singular story of their house demonstrates, in that Aquarian Age of doing your own thing, the Sallicks were suburban Flower Children, marching to the beat of a different drum.

"We were *the contrarians*," Barbara says of her and Robert's passion for eighteenth-century furniture and objects, which they began collecting shortly after marriage. "We both sort of liked it, that we'd landed on something we enjoyed doing together. And when you have beautiful antiques, you want to put them in a house that fits." For the Sallicks, that meant Colonial, and of the original vintage. "There was a craftsmanship to the eighteenth-century houses we visited that we loved—the beautiful old windows and floors, the warmth of the materials, the simple details. And we wanted the complete environment for our collection."

It was a dream that proved hard to realize. "We looked at tons of places, and they were all in various states of falling down," Barbara recalls of their house-hunting excursions, which often included her father, a no-nonsense man who employed Robert in the family business. "He was a very 'what are you doing?' kind of guy," says his daughter, "and he'd find something wrong with every house. And finally after saying 'are you nuts?' for the hundredth time, my father suggested that we build."

That was, of course, precisely what the Sallicks didn't want to do—until the couple hit on a novel way of doing it. Rather than hiring an architect, they went to Washington, D.C. "Someone had told us that, as part of the Works Progress Administration in the 1930s, unemployed architects had gone all over Connecticut and Massachusetts and meticulously documented a number of really beautiful eighteenth-century houses," Barbara says. "So we decided to have a look." The plans were housed in the Library of Congress, where the couple found two similar structures, both in Wethersfield, Connecticut, of particular appeal: the eighteenth-century Joseph Webb and Silas Deane houses (both now a part of the Webb-Deane-Stevens Museum in Wethersfield). Though the buildings weren't identical to one another, "there was a consistency to them, including the proportions, the rake of the roof, the kinds of doors—so many things that were typical of the style of the period," Barbara says. "We bought two sets of plans—*complete* sets, down to the last molding—for twenty dollars apiece." Thus armed, the Sallicks approached the Bedford, New York architect Livingston Elder, and asked him to conflate the Webb and Deane designs into a "contemporary historic" home that would be at once authentically in period and entirely suited to the needs of a postwar American family.

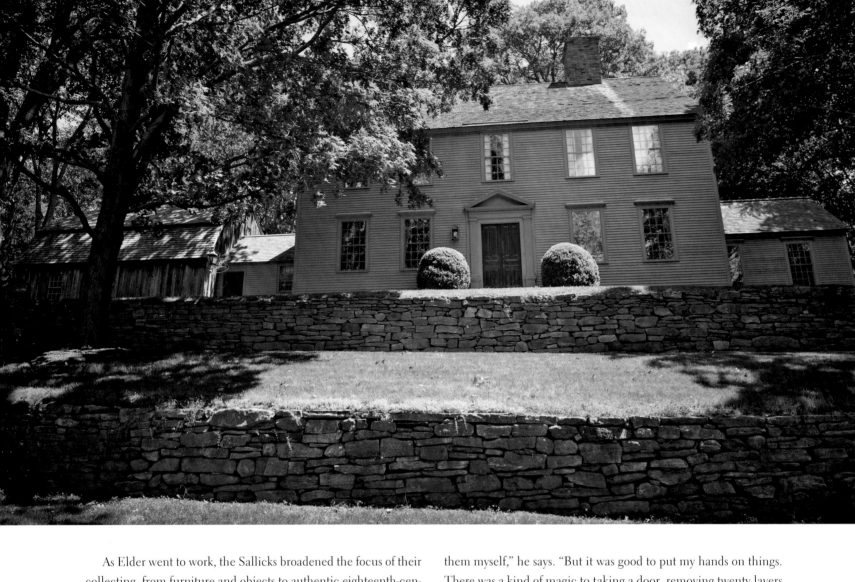

As Elder went to work, the Sallicks broadened the focus of their collecting, from furniture and objects to authentic eighteenth-century architectural components—doors and their frames, hardware, floorboards, entire paneled walls, mantelpieces, even bricks. "Livingston measured all the parts we bought and worked them into the design—he put the whole house together like a big puzzle," Barbara explains. To iron out the temporal wrinkles, the couple engaged a carpenter named Clarke Fancher—they characterize him as more of a craftsman—who cut and adjusted the elements, such as the doors. "The width of each doorway was different, but the heights had to be consistent, and some of them were too short," Robert explains. "So Clarke added pieces to the bottoms—he put on elevator shoes." Oftentimes Fancher and Robert worked side by side. "It took 816 antique nails to hang all of the shutters—I know, because I straightened every one of

them myself," he says. "But it was good to put my hands on things. There was a kind of magic to taking a door, removing twenty layers of paint, and discovering all the details."

What emerged, finally, was a structure that, while unmistakably of its time, seems to belong with equal authenticity to history, to the plainspoken tapestry of Colonial architecture that overlays the American northeast. The 32-by-40-foot footprint of the core structure (excluding the barn-style garage/office and greenhouse-turned-den) was an eighteenth-century standard, and the layout is what Barbara describes as "foursquare—four rooms downstairs, four up, all more or less fourteen-by-sixteen, with a broad central hall connecting the front and back doors." There are two chimneys—one on each side of the house—so that the four first-floor spaces (dining room and kitchen, living and family rooms) have fireplaces, as does the upstairs master

ABOVE & OPPOSITE: While the house was in design, the Sallicks searched for Colonial-era components, which their architect, Livingston Elder, worked into the plan.

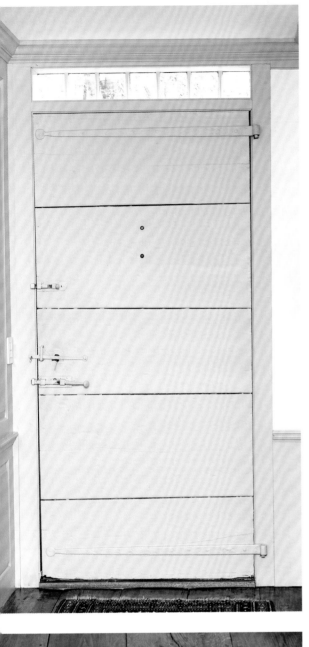

suite. "And the house is built like an eighteenth-century house would have been built," she explains. "First all the trim went in, and the wainscot and moldings. Then after everything was in place, the plasterer came and did the walls."

All of the wood, the Sallicks claim, is in period—not only the wide-plank heart pine and chestnut floors ("hand-scraped and waxed, not sanded"), but also the wall boards, which Fancher cut to fit. The center hall features the low wainscoting typical of Colonial architecture, and the paneled walls in the living and dining rooms were installed intact—though as they were originally built for slightly shorter spaces, Elder designed pieces to fill in the gaps between wall and ceiling. Adding strongly to the house's character is the hardware, all of which was stripped and repainted in the Colonial manner and compels on close examination the same fascination one feels instinctively for old flintlocks and timepieces. As with other of the house's components, the hardware's diminutive scale contributes to an overall lack of ostentation, to a simplicity that feels philosophically connected to the ideals of Early American life.

Not everything, of course, is original, yet even in new or hybrid elements the interleaving of historic and contemporary appears seamless. "Everything on the stair is new except the treads," Barbara says. "But we found a spindle baluster that we liked, and a very skilled stair builder who copied it and installed everything." "The wainscot on the stair is actually old paneling," Robert adds. "We might have shortened it a bit to fit the space."

In the end, the Sallicks' gambit benefited from the remarkable consistency of Colonial proportions and architectural elements, which amounted to a version of modular construction. "The front door came from somewhere in upstate Connecticut around Berlin, and the stone front steps belonged to a house that was built in Danbury, and they fit together perfectly," Barbara says, still marveling. "How did we ever find such things?"

As things turned out, the couple's adventure in mixing the historic and contemporary, the authentic and designed, didn't end with their home. In 1972, having harvested considerable knowledge and experience, Barbara quit teaching and became an assistant curator in the department of American decorative arts at the Yale University Art Gallery. Six years after that, she and Robert combined his knowledge of plumbing and engineering and their joint passion for well-designed quotidian objects and began Waterworks, the company that helped transform the American perception of the bathroom from a place to do your business into a luxurious, personalized living space. If, in 1978, that seemed like a fantastical concept, the Sallicks were, as ever, following their different drummer; and eventually the marketplace fell lucratively into step.

The Sallick residence is not, strictly speaking, an old house that has received a new life, but rather a more flexible interpretation of the idea: a modern structure based on two specific examples of a historic typology, constructed from components that, drawing on an array of sources, forms a lapidary collage of eighteenth-century architectural iconography. The kitchen and baths aside, the house also remains a very particular interpretation of history. While the Sallicks were indeed contrarian in turning, in 1968, against the prevailing preference for contemporary Scandinavian design, it's worth noting that the origins of Danish Modern can be found in the craft traditions of earlier centuries, and the Sallicks' house, with its material richness and limited palette of simple details and unfussy period furnishings ("Boston, not Philadelphia," in Robert's formulation) reflects a postwar sensibility—call it Colonial Modern.

"It was just one component of what I'd call a circular life," Barbara says of the house—a life that embraced travel, lectures, and museum-going devoted to the Sallicks' shared aesthetic interests; their highly successful global brand, one that draws on vintage bath fittings and fixtures to enable a mass audience to enjoy contemporary pleasures rooted in nostalgic associations; and even allowed the couple to instill in their children an appreciation of, and respect for, quality in design and architecture. Not least, there is the *bella figura*, the notion of what your home says about you, and how its architecture suggests the embrace of certain values and rejection of others.

Thus the Sallicks have what might be described as a "purpose-built" historic home, the purpose being not only the pursuit of style or shelter, but the desire to use the past to build a future—an excellent way to extract a new life from an old house, and one that, decades after America lowered its freak flag and slunk back into conformity, still endures.

PRECEDING SPREAD: The stair combines antique treads and paneling (cut to fit) with new balusters based on a historic one the couple admired. A long crack distinguishes a reclaimed floorboard.

OPPOSITE: Wanting a period-appropriate setting for their antique furniture collection, the Sallicks found Colonial-era doors, casings, wainscoting, and entire paneled walls.

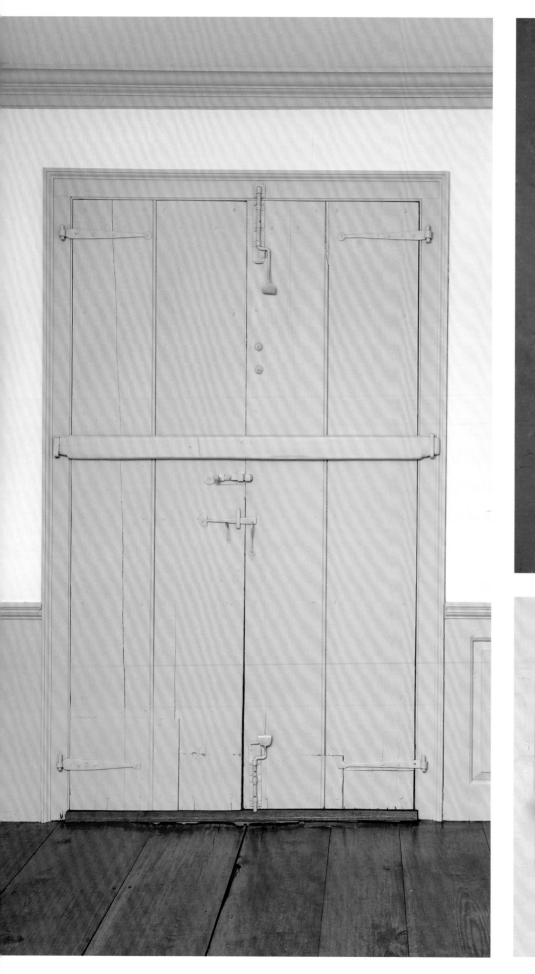

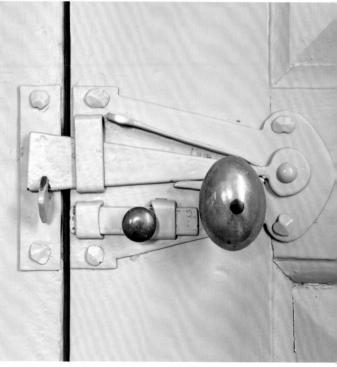

OPPOSITE: Much of the hardware was stripped and repainted according to Colonial custom. RIGHT: When new construction was unavoidable, the carpenter, Clarke Fancher, used old wood. Robert Sallick found the eighteenth-century bricks and oversaw their arrangement.

15

WHITE HOUSE
isle of coll, scotland

"WHAT IS IT THAT ATTRACTS PEOPLE TO RUINS?" asks the Edinburgh-based architect William Tunnell rhetorically. "I think it's a sense of history, context, character, and charm. And," he adds, "a ruin tells a story. And it was important, on this project, not to airbrush that story out."

The history of the White House, on the Isle of Coll in Scotland's Inner Hebrides, is rich and colorful, as is that of the place itself. "Now it's quite comfortable, but two hundred years ago, life was unimaginably difficult, given the extremes of weather and how remote it is," Tunnell says of Coll, a thirteen-by-four-mile island about three hours by ferry west of Oban, on the Firth of Lorn. Tunnell's assurances notwithstanding, there remains an overlay of atavism: a patch of rough weather can suspend all transportation and leave a traveler stranded—and with a lot of downtime. Coll's website is comical in its cheerful assurances of boredom and inactivity: Other than enjoying the island's natural beauty, the interested tourist is informed that "there is almost nowhere to stay and nothing to do once here!"

Grishipol House, as the Georgian residence was originally called, grew out of Scotland's change in the nature of land ownership, from clans to individuals. It was built in the mid-1700s for the tack man, the agent charged with collecting rents from the tenant farmers for the laird, or landowner. Though the original building wasn't all that big—"the footprint is probably seventy-five square meters," the architect estimates—"it was very grand compared to the local two-room dwellings—the first lime-built, square-cornered, slate-roofed building on Coll." Significantly, Grishipol House was also white-washed, which set it apart from the farmer's typical "black house," so called for the soot that emerged from the hole in the roof

OPPOSITE: As the people of the Isle of Coll cherished the White House's iconic fissured gable, architect William Tunnell took pains to stabilize and preserve (rather than repair) the damage.

through which fire smoke ventilated. When exactly the tack man moved on is hard to pinpoint, but "there are records that the house may have been used as a tweed mill, and about a hundred years after its construction it became unoccupied," Tunnell says. "By the late 1800s, it was a full ruin."

Tunnell's clients, a couple with three children, inherited the site from the husband's family, "and had been farming the land, staying in a nearby house they didn't own, and wanted to build," the architect recalls. "They were drawn to the location—relatively level and dry, on a stand-alone bay—and were considering all options, from restoring the White House to building a separate structure near it." On an early site visit, Tunnell asked the couple what they most liked about the setting. "They said, 'We like the ruin'—and I pointed out that, if they fixed it up, they wouldn't have it as a ruin anymore." As an alternative, the architect proposed that "they have their ruin and eat it too, by occupying a part of it but maintaining the most dramatically cleft part as a roofless courtyard." In fact, the outcome includes three elements: the original structure, half of which is open courtyard as planned, the rest given to a ground-floor kitchen and upstairs master suite and study, united by a contemporary glass, steel, and oak stair rising up from the entry hall; a fully glazed one-story volume that serves as the open-plan living/dining area; and a new two-story wing, with a partially enclosed informal study area, a library in a circulation corridor, and four bedrooms.

Before the plan could be executed, however, the structure had to be stabilized. While the three cross-walls and two gable walls were intact, Tunnell describes the house's overall condition as "chunky and gnarly. The dramatic disintegration probably was fairly quick, and happened when the roof timbers gave way, and the weight of

LEFT & OPPOSITE:
Though they wanted
a habitable home, it was
the uninhabitable ruin to
which the owners were
attracted. Accordingly,
Tunnell preserved (and
only partly programmed)
the original, constructed
an architecturally
sympathetic wing, and
united the two with a fully
glazed living/dining room.

the roof pushed the walls apart." The biggest problem, the architect reveals, was that the building had no foundation and sat on sand, which had been excavated by treasure-hunters. "The folklore on the island was that there was gold buried under the walls, and people had dug under the corners looking for it," Tunnell relates. "Whether or not the gold story is true I couldn't say—*I* didn't find any."

The major preservation issue involved the southern gable wall, with its alarming top-to-bottom fissure, which had "left the chimney defying gravity," Tunnell says. The damage had also, paradoxically, become the White House's signature, and so "the primary challenge in solidifying the ruin was making sure the wall was made secure—and that the process of making it secure didn't bring it down."

Each component of the house received a specific treatment. "The walls of the original building were three or four feet thick, so the rooms inside were very small and cellular, and the ceiling heights were extraordinarily low," Tunnell recalls. The new construction occupies the northern part of the ruin, preserving the old front door, which opens into a surprisingly light and airy formal entry hall—"it's an outside-y sort of space," the architect explains. Though the new floor-to-ceiling heights "are suited to contemporary living and contemporary-sized people," he says, "you can still see the sockets in the walls where the timbers were—the tiny windows, the fireplaces at different heights—so you keep a sense of what the building was."

If the glass-enclosed living/dining element is clearly contemporary, the new wing beyond it offers more of an aesthetic mix of the modern and the vernacular. The irregularly stacked stone of its western wall, which extends slightly into the landscape at both ends, references the White House's period construction, with the down-sloping roof nearly touching the top of it—"it's a bit like a sou'wester hat and exposes as little neck as possible," Tunnell says. "The idea is to create a traditional sense of protection and enclosure. A lot of that is psychological," he adds, "because they do get hurricane-force winds there and the timber frame buildings do just fine." By contrast, "everything else is used to enclose space, and is cleanly detailed and skinned—black timber, glass, and whitewashed walls."

The difference between traditional and contemporary construction—between what could be asked of a building two centuries ago and how it can perform today—expresses what is, in the architect's view, the White House's most interesting connection to the past. "When the place was first built, it was much harder to keep the weather out, and they didn't have the technology for big picture windows," Tunnell says. "So the house was sited in a picturesque place and was meant to be a picturesque object on the landscape. Today that's been turned inside out by the availability of large expanses of glass, transforming the building into a place from which to view beautiful things." Thus the White House embodies both the historic notion of

the object that completes the view and the contemporary idea of the view as seen from the object.

Like many architects who work with existing structures, Tunnell is grateful to have the collaboration of history. "We often describe what we do as 'responsive architecture,'" he says. "Rather than imposing a preconceived idea that you drop on the site and then admire, we respond to a range of specifics—physical, operational, emotional, and some that are hard to define." With the White House, "the starting point was to have a clarity between new and old, and to avoid pastiche—to make informed choices between restoring and re-creating things, which you want to avoid because it takes away from the story." Indeed, uncovering the

ABOVE: An informal study area, off the living/dining space, in the new wing.
OPPOSITE: A new grand stair, in the southern part of the ruin, preserves its voluminous character and leaves the original apertures and details exposed.

story lies at the heart of contending with the past. "I've never liked anything more than just walking around a building and trying to determine why things are the way they are. That's why the tourist industry is so good in Scotland—there are lots of good tales, and lots of old buildings to tell them about."

Most important, Tunnell believes, is to remember that buildings—whether old or new, houses or otherwise—are living things. "It's not about pickling something in aspic, and admiring it as an artifact," he says. "If we hadn't found a way to occupy the White House, it would have fallen down eventually. We came up with a compromise—otherwise it would have been lost."

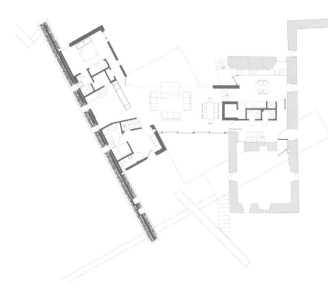

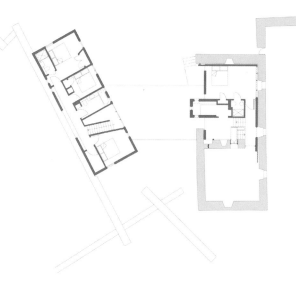

ABOVE: A stacked stone
wall encloses the new
wing, and extends
past it into the land-
scape, conveying
a sense of protection
and enclosure.

OPPOSITE: A second-
floor hallway in the new
wing doubles as a library
and frames the rough,
majestic view.

PHOTO CREDITS

THE NEW OLD HOUSE

William Abranowicz
Cover

Courtesy of Acme
28, 29 btm, 37 btm

Jean Allsopp
112, 116, 118, 120, 121
top, 122, 123, 124–128,
130, 131

Photo: Iwan Baan
12 top, 190 top, 192 top,
194, 196 rt, 197 top, 199,
200, 202 btm

Benjamin Benschneider/
Olson Kundig
150 btm rt

Hélène Binet
56, 58, 61 lft, 63

Joakim Boren
94, 96 top, 98, 100, 101
top, 102, 104–111

Darren Bradley
190 btm, 205, 207, 208
top, 209–214

© James Brittain Photography
174, 178 btm, 179, 180,
182, 183, 186, 187

Lee Dunnette
11 btm

Torben Eskerod
9 lft

© Elizabeth Felicella/Esto
74, 77, 80 top, 81, 82, 83
top, 86, 87

Photo © Mark Fiennes/
BridgemanImages
162

Alex Franklin Photography
165–168, 171 top, 173

Courtesy of Found Associates
138 top

FRENCH + TYE
185, 188

Adam Friedberg
40 lft, 50–55 top

Courtesy of Fuster +
Architects
19 btm, 25 btm

Nataniel Fuster-Felix
21

© J. Paul Getty Trust.
Getty Research Institute,
Los Angeles (2004.R.10)
196 lft, 198, 201, 202 top,
203

Courtesy of James Gorst
Architects Ltd
170 top, 171 btm

Courtesy of Allan Greenberg
Architect LLC
90 btm

Michael Harding
229 btm, 236, back cover

David Hill
114

Courtesy of HILLWORKS
115, 117, 121 btm

Sloan T Howard Photography/
www.sthphoto.com
216, 218, 221, 222 btm,
224, 225

Hufton & Crow
134, 135 top, 139

John Ike
208 btm, 215

Michael Jensen/
Olson Kundig
150 rt mid, 152, 153

Dean Kaufman/
Trunk Archive
13 btm

Christian Kerber
11 top

Raimund Koch
5, 16, 18, 19 top, 22–24,
25 top

Courtesy of Olson Kundig
149 btm, 150 lft

Andrew Lee
226, 229 top, 230, 232,
233 top, 234, 235

Courtesy of Adrian
Leeper-Bueno
55 btm

Copyright Lincoln Center
for the Performing Arts
12 btm

Dirk Lindner
Front leaf, 177, 181 top,
184

Courtesy of Lorcan O'Herlihy
Architects
192 btm, 197 btm

Courtesy of LTL Architects
42 rt, 46 btm, 47 btm

Mark Luscombe-Whyte/
The Interior Archive
169, 170 btm, 172

Andrew Merideth
132, 135 btm, 136, 138
btm, 140, 142, 145

James Merrel
137, 144

© The Metropolitan Museum
of Art. Image source:
Art Resource, NY
13 top

© Sir John Soane's Museum,
London 2016. Photo:
Derry Moore
14 lft

Michael Moran/
Architectural Digest,
July 2010/Condé Nast
90 top, 92

Michael Moran/OTTO
40 rt, 42 lft, 43, 44, 46
top, 47 top, 48, 88, 93

Jaime Navarro
4, 20

Jim Olson/Olson Kundig
150 top, 151

Courtesy of Messana O'Rorke
76, 80 btm

Cristobal Palma/Estudio
Palma
Title page, 26, 29 top, 30,
32–37 top, 38, 39

Photos: Costas Picadas
78, 83 btm, 84, 85

Photo: Kevin Scott
7, 146, 148, 149 top,
154, 155, 156 btm, 157,
158–160, case

Courtesy of David Sheppard
Architects
96 btm, 97

Image courtesy of Hoerr
Schaudt Landscape
Architects, Photographer:
Scott Shigley
91

Anna Stathaki
178 top

www.timeincukcontent.com/
Ngoc Ming Ngo
219, 220, 222 top

Courtesy of Jonathan
Tuckey Design
176, 181 btm

Veyko
49

Philip Vile
59, 61 rt, 62, 64–68,
70–73

William Waldron
204, 206

Courtesy of Witherford
Watson Mann
60

Courtesy of WT Architecture
228, 233 btm

© Nigel Young/
Foster + Partners
9 rt

Liao Yusheng
14 rt

ACKNOWLEDGMENTS

THIS BOOK OWES ITS EXISTENCE to two people. The first is Andrea Danese, my original editor: Andrea helped me to refine the concept; vetted the projects I selected and made her own excellent suggestions; kept the faith through what turned out to be several years of publishing limbo; and finally got the book up and running, miracle of miracles. The second person is Elizabeth Hyland, who oversaw the selection and acquisition of all the photography and visual elements: Lizzy kept track of voluminous amounts of material, handled the traffic management expertly, dealt with all the personalities tactfully, and did it cheerfully, tirelessly, and uncomplainingly.

Andrea, Lizzy—you have all my gratitude. This book is as much yours as mine.

It's also my pleasure to thank the book's imaginative designer, Sarah Gifford. *The New Old House* drew on multiple sources for its visual material, with the result that there was no consistency of style or quality. Sarah brought everything expertly, elegantly into balance, and devised motifs that supported the subject and, not least, resulted in a beautiful outcome.

I must also mention the UK-based writer and editor Jonathan Bell, who led me to a number of projects, and whose contribution to this book cannot be overstated – thank you, Jonathan.

The architects and homeowners (sometimes one and the same) whose residences are in this book were, without exception, generous with their time, expertise, and support, and welcomed me into their homes unreservedly. I am very grateful for all they taught me, and the kindness they showed me. Thanks to you all.

My gratitude as well to the photographers whose work appears in these pages. Some of them I didn't meet; others extended themselves considerably to make sure that the projects were well represented. All of them, as you have seen, do excellent work.

I was fortunate to have the interest and encouragement of an exceptional team at Abrams. My thanks to Michael Sand, the publisher; the optimistic and resourceful Shawna Mullen, who followed Andrea Danese as editor; Mary Hern, director of managing editorial; Erin Slonaker, my copy editor; and Drew Wheeler, who proofread the finished text. To write a book like this is a privilege, and I am deeply grateful to Abrams for giving it to me.

Across nearly thirty books, I have had the good fortune to work with Jill Cohen. It's easiest to say that she's my agent, but that isn't entirely accurate, and it doesn't begin to describe everything she's done, which includes giving me my start in the world of illustrated books; encouraging multiple architects and designers to work with me; advising me tirelessly on every matter pertaining to business, and quite a few pertaining to life; and most of all, being my friend. The ocean of Jill's hard work, knowledge, experience, taste, and good cheer has floated more boats than can be counted. We all love and cherish her, no one more than myself.

I would like to thank as well my father-in-law, James Ackerman, for the interest he has taken in what I do, the help he has extended, and for the example of his life's work. And, too, my wife, Anne, who has cheered me on, encouraged me when I lost confidence, and given me the gift of her singular personality.

Finally, this book is dedicated to my father, Keeva, who is with me every day, and has proven the adage that death ends a life but not a relationship; and to my mother, Bebe, who always tries her hardest in all matters, and who never met an old house that she couldn't make new.

editor: SHAWNA MULLEN

designer: SARAH GIFFORD

production manager: ANET SIRNA-BRUDER

photo research: LIZZY HYLAND

Library of Congress Control Number: 2016945896

ISBN: 978-1-4197-2404-6

Text copyright © 2017 Marc Kristal
Foreword copyright © 2017 Gil Schafer III

Published in 2017 by Abrams, an imprint of ABRAMS. All rights reserved.
No portion of this book may be reproduced, stored in a retrieval system, or transmitted
in any form or by any means, mechanical, electronic, photocopying, recording,
or otherwise, without written permission from the publisher.

Printed and bound in China
10 9 8 7 6 5 4 3 2 1

Abrams books are available at special discounts when purchased in quantity
for premiums and promotions as well as fundraising or educational use.
Special editions can also be created to specification.
For details, contact specialsales@abramsbooks.com or the address below.

ABRAMS The Art of Books
115 West 18th Street, New York, NY 10011
abramsbooks.com